JEFFERSON, LINCOLN,
AND THE UNFINISHED WORK OF THE NATION

{ Ronald L. Hatzenbuehler }

JEFFERSON, LINCOLN,

AND THE UNFINISHED
WORK OF THE NATION

Southern Illinois University Press
Carbondale

19 18 17 16   4 3 2 1

Cover design: Shawn M. Tarr
Cover illustration: photograph of Mount Rushmore National
  Memorial from Wikimedia Commons; photographer,
  Kimon Berlin.

Library of Congress Cataloging-in-Publication Data
Names: Hatzenbuehler, Ronald L., author.
Title: Jefferson, Lincoln, and the unfinished work of the nation /
  Ronald L. Hatzenbuehler.
Description: Carbondale : Southern Illinois University Press,
  2016. | Includes bibliographical references and index.
Identifiers: LCCN 2015037060| ISBN 9780809334902 (pbk. :
  alk. paper) | ISBN 9780809334919 (e-book)
Subjects: LCSH: Jefferson, Thomas, 1743–1826—Political and
  social views. | Lincoln, Abraham, 1809–1865—Political and
  social views. | United States—Politics and government—
  19th century—Philosophy. | United States—Politics and
  government—Philosophy.
Classification: LCC E332.2 .H39 2016 | DDC 973.4/6092—
  dc23 LC record available at http://lccn.loc.gov/2015037060

Printed on recycled paper. ♻

This paper meets the requirements of ANSI/NISO
Z39.48-1992 (Permanence of Paper) ∞

To Eva and Miles

{ Contents }

{ Illustrations }

---------------------------------{ Acknowledgments }---------------------------------

I embrace the opportunity to thank those individuals whose advice and support facilitated completing this writing project. It owes its maturation to programming underwritten by the Idaho Humanities Council (IHC), beginning in the summer of 2004 with its annual Teachers' Institute devoted to the presidency of Thomas Jefferson ("An Unfinished Revolution"). At the time, I was completing a study—subsequently published as *"I Tremble for My Country": Thomas Jefferson and the Virginia Gentry*—that emphasized the fact that Jefferson was an uneasy member of Virginia gentry because he both participated in the privileges that group enjoyed and episodically criticized its behaviors.[1] Because it is impossible to study his presidency in isolation from his other life experiences, our discussions that summer meandered into many meadows and were guided throughout by attention to the exceptional power of Jefferson's phrasing of his ideas to escape the bounds of his time. We concluded that his words—but not in every case his actions—are powerful references for the nation's unfinished work of creating a society in which everyone is equal before the law.

During the next couple of years, I became involved in the run-up to bicentennial celebrations of Abraham Lincoln's birth (2009). Although I had purchased the nine-volume set of *The Collected Works of Abraham Lincoln* as a graduate student (as a promotional gift for joining the History Book Club), my knowledge of his writings and speeches was limited essentially to snippets from the Lincoln-Douglas debates and his major addresses. To deepen my understanding of Lincoln's life, I assigned Michael P. Johnson's *Abraham Lincoln, Slavery, and the Civil War: Selected Writings and Speeches* to the students in my introductory US history survey courses so that with them I could study him anew.[2]

Then, in the summer of 2006, the IHC devoted its Teachers' Institute to Lincoln's presidency ("Controlled by Events"). Although our primary focus was Lincoln's decisions during the Civil War, the fact that many of the teachers had attended the previous institute on Jefferson's presidency led to provocative discussions exploring how Lincoln frequently viewed the events of his time through the lens of the nation's founding principles. From discussions with the participants at the Teachers' Institutes and with my students, I formulated similarities and differences in the thoughts and actions of the two individuals and began to think that an extended comparison of their ideas in certain areas might be worthwhile.

As my interest in this topic grew, I was surprised to learn that few books or articles place the two men side by side. I found books that address them separately in the same volume, such as Richard Hofstadter's classic *The American Political Tradition and the Men Who Made It*; that trace the evolution of an idea from the Revolutionary period through the Civil War, such as Sean Wilentz's *The Rise of American Democracy: Jefferson to Lincoln*; or that investigate one specific topic, such as Everett Eugene Edwards's *Washington, Jefferson, Lincoln and Agriculture*.[3] Merrill D. Peterson would seem to have been uniquely qualified to undertake such an endeavor because of his books addressing changing views on the two men over time, but he limited his comparisons to Jefferson's and Lincoln's contemporaries.[4] Aside from a small pamphlet that Pulitzer Prize–winning editorialist F. Lauriston Bullard authored in 1948, I know of no lengthy direct juxtapositions.[5]

I presented a version of chapter 4 in 2003 at the Fifth International Conference of the Lincoln Center for American Studies at LSU–Shreveport under the title "Choosing Thomas Jefferson." In October 2008, I presented my initial views of the importance of place for Jefferson and Lincoln at the annual meeting of the Idaho Council of Teacher Education, and I wrote a formal, academic paper devoted to the topic for the Virginia Forum the following year (a revised version appears as the epilogue). That fall semester, I offered an upper-level course on Jefferson and Lincoln, relying on their primary sources, and I delivered a talk the following spring to the Idaho State University (ISU) chapter of Phi Kappa Phi (the national science fraternity), comparing and contrasting the two men's educational ideas (chapter 6 is a revised portion of this talk). In fall 2009, the IHC honored me with a research fellowship supporting this book project.

From 2012 to 2014, I participated in IHC-sponsored public discussions during bicentennial commemorations of the Civil War, and I saw firsthand the interest that adults have in topics related to that war's origins (stretching back to the founding period), development, and aftermath. To my delight, most audiences rejected facile conclusions that "the North won the war" or Pollyannaish thinking that "everything turned out all right in the end" and instead chose to delve deeply into the implications of the war for today's society. I was especially gratified to see that individuals who either embrace or reject the notion of American exceptionalism—the belief that the United States has a unique history and that its founding ideals are worthy of emulation by other nations—could come together to study how the war continues to divide Americans with respect to its meanings for the nation.[6]

Throughout my investigation and writing, I have been guided by the IHC's mission, "to deepen understanding of human experience by connecting people with ideas." In addition, I have tried to balance the fact that I address topics from an avowedly academic perspective rooted in the two men's writings and speeches with a strong belief that the contents of the book should appeal to a general reading audience rather than exclusively to practicing historians. In writing the book primarily for nonspecialists, I have adhered to admonitions that historians should eschew jargon and narrowly focused topics of interest to only a few in favor of reader-friendly prose devoted to issues of import.

I am especially indebted to IHC executive director Rick Ardinger, his staff (especially Cindy Wang), and the IHC board of directors for their continuing support, including opening the pages of *Idaho Humanities* to my musings on various topics associated with writing the book.[7] In addition to IHC's sponsorship, other groups have provided me with audiences with which to work through the book's logic, including New Knowledge Adventures, an offshoot of Elderhostel sponsored by the Continuing Education Program at Idaho State University (my thanks go especially to its program director, Dr. Bill Brydon); the Sagebrush Society, a small group of civic-minded individuals that meets monthly to discuss books and topics of interest to its members; and various civic clubs.

In addition, I gratefully acknowledge the contributions of colleagues and friends. Political scientist David Gray Adler codirected the Teacher Institutes; he has taught me much about constitutional issues surrounding the presidencies of Jefferson and Lincoln, as well as suggesting nuanced readings of their texts. Attendees at annual meetings of the Front Range Early American Consortium (FREACs), particularly Mick Nicholls, Ken Lockridge, and Billy Smith, have offered wise comments on versions of several chapters. I'm especially thankful to Billy for allowing me to invite myself to Montana State University in fall 2014 to present chapter 1 to his graduate seminar in early American history.

Other historians who deserve special acknowledgment are Charley Killinger, whose friendship dates to our undergraduate days, and Bill Hine, a close friend from graduate school. Charley began his graduate studies in early America before turning to Italian history and taught both subjects until his recent retirement. Bill is a specialist in African American history and, with Darlene Clark Hine, joined Dave Adler and me for the Teachers' Institute devoted to Lincoln's presidency. I thank these associates not only for their friendships, which now extend across several decades, but also for their willingness to offer consistently high-quality reflections on what seems to work and what does not.

Billy Carter, a retired attorney from North Carolina who has settled in Pocatello, has read a version of most of the book and has challenged me to rethink my conclusions in numerous areas. Son Patrick, a doctoral student in agricultural economics at Purdue University, offered especially beneficial advice on the introduction and chapter 6, along with former student John Bailey Jr. I am also indebted to two anonymous readers for Southern Illinois University Press, the production staff at the press, and especially editor Sylvia Frank Rodrigue, for her advice and patience with me throughout the writing process. Mark Neels at the Papers of Abraham Lincoln kindly reviewed the manuscript and provided valuable advice on content and phrasing.

I am dedicating the book to our grandchildren, Eva and Miles, not because they did anything tangible to aid in its composition but with my hope that it might spark an interest in history. They've already met TJ; now they'll meet AL.

JEFFERSON, LINCOLN,
AND THE UNFINISHED WORK OF THE NATION

---------------------------------{ Introduction }------------------------------------

Thomas Jefferson and Abraham Lincoln occupy distinctive places in American memory. Their monuments in the nation's capital annually attract millions of visitors (7 million to the Lincoln Memorial in 2014, the largest number of visitors to any Washington, DC, site, and 2.7 million to the Jefferson Memorial), and their faces adorn another popular US tourist attraction, Mount Rushmore (2.1 million visitors in 2014).[1] Scholarly opinion of their importance as national leaders coincides, as books addressing the two men's lives and legacies continue to be written, and their names routinely appear on lists of the "top five" US presidents.

A key element in the importance accorded to Jefferson and Lincoln relates to their writings, selections from which adorn their memorials. The four heavily edited panels at Jefferson's Memorial emphasize his commitment to freedom for the nation from British control (*A Summary View of the Rights of British America* and the Declaration of Independence); freedom of conscience (Virginia Statute for Religious Freedom) and the mind through public education; and freedom for enslaved individuals. At the Lincoln Memorial, visitors can read the full texts of the Gettysburg Address and the second inaugural address. The former summoned the nation to engage in "a new birth of freedom"; the latter, to "achieve and cherish a just and lasting peace, among ourselves, and with all nations." On Lincoln's birthday in 1939, a crowd of seventy-five thousand heard renowned contralto Marian Anderson sing "My Country 'Tis of Thee" from the steps of the Memorial, her appearance at Constitution Hall having been blocked by the Daughters of the American Revolution; and in August 1963, Dr. Martin Luther King Jr. reminded over two hundred thousand listeners that the words of

1

The Lincoln Memorial, which more visitors annually seek out than any other site in Washington, DC. *Carol M. Highsmith, photographer, "Aerial View of the Lincoln Memorial, Washington, D.C." Carol M. Highsmith Collection, Library of Congress.*

freedom contained in the nation's founding documents remained unfulfilled for African Americans.[2]

Despite the close proximity of the Jefferson and Lincoln Memorials, the similarities in content of the writings adorning their interior spaces, and the esteem accorded to both individuals, it is surprising that scholars have devoted few pages to comparing their ideas and actions regarding how the United States should develop as a nation. One is more likely to see Jefferson compared with Alexander Hamilton; Lincoln, with Jefferson Davis. One explanation for this lack of head-to-head comparison is that these two prominent Americans lived in separate time periods. Admittedly, comparing two people whose lives did not intersect presents challenges, but these challenges are not insurmountable, and such a comparison is valuable and important for three primary reasons.

First, in his speeches after 1854, Lincoln frequently drew direct parallels between his era, labeled as "the crisis of the 1850s" by current historians, and the critical period surrounding the nation's founding. He looked back to the founders and their writings to form his own ideas of what the nation might become. With respect specifically to slavery, Lincoln argued

that Jefferson and other founders had placed the institution on the road
to extinction by passing the Northwest Ordinance (1787), which contained
a clause from Jefferson's 1784 bill that slavery be forbidden in that area;
not mentioning slavery specifically in the Constitution; and enacting the
Missouri Compromise, which limited slavery's expansion into lands of
the Louisiana Purchase above Missouri's southern boundary (36°30′).
When Congress passed the Kansas-Nebraska Act, Lincoln accused Americans of his generation of rejecting the views of the founders in favor of
economic self-interest.

He also challenged Stephen Douglas's belief that the Declaration of
Independence created a nation exclusively for white men. In response,
Lincoln repeatedly affirmed that he drew all of his civic sentiments from
the Declaration of Independence and asserted that African Americans
were entitled to the same rights to "life, liberty, and the pursuit of happiness" that whites enjoyed.[3] When Douglas attempted to counter Lincoln's
interpretation of the Declaration's "unalienable rights" with the fact that
Jefferson was a slaveholder and therefore would never have meant to include African Americans under the document, Lincoln responded that
Jefferson at several points in his life had written disapprovingly of slavery
and sought to abolish the practice in Virginia (see chapter 1). Lincoln also
accused Southerners living in the 1850s of declension from Jefferson's beliefs by quoting from their texts where they referred to the language of the
Declaration as "glittering generalities" and "self evident lies" or asserted
that Jefferson's writings applied only to "superior races." "[S]oberly," he
wrote in an 1859 letter declining an invitation to attend a celebration of
Jefferson's birth, "it is now no child's play to save the principles of Jefferson
from total overthrow in this nation."[4]

Most directly, as president, Lincoln justified his decision to call Congress
into special session on July 4, 1861 (see chapter 3), by writing that the government of the United States was an ongoing experiment. The American
Revolution had established the nation; the adoption of the Constitution,
along with the subsequent ratification of the Bill of Rights, had led to its
successful administration; and the Civil War was testing whether it could
be maintained during an attempt to overthrow it. Then, in the Gettysburg
Address, Lincoln reminded his listeners that the Civil War was returning
the nation to the principles of 1776 by asking them to count backward from
1863 for "[f]our score and seven years." He also told them that the soldiers

who fell at the Battle of Gettysburg gave their "last full measure of devotion" to their nation, ensuring that its founding ideals would not die.[5]

Second, both Lincoln and Jefferson felt that the work of the nation begun at its founding remained unfinished. The title of this book—borrowed from the Gettysburg Address—builds on Lincoln's admonition that the sacrifice of the soldiers who died at the Battle of Gettysburg was yet incomplete because the nation had not achieved the full measure of the Declaration's promise of unalienable rights. By the fall of 1863, Lincoln was moving toward ending slavery in the nation (see chapter 1), and he used the small space accorded him at Gettysburg to call the nation "to be dedicated here to the *unfinished work* which they who fought here have so nobly advanced."[6]

Then, in the closing section of his second inaugural address, Lincoln broadened the meaning of "unfinished work" to include more than just an end to slavery. As the Civil War was coming to a close, the president reminded his hearers that it was yet necessary to "strive on to *finish the work* we are in."[7] This sentiment that the nation had not completed the work that it had begun in 1776 also well encapsulates Jefferson's life. For example, in one of the last letters that he wrote (Lincoln may have alluded to this letter in his of 1859 quoted above), Jefferson expressed the hope that Americans would annually rededicate themselves to protecting the rights expressed in the Declaration of Independence and that people everywhere would eventually "assume the blessings and security of self-government."[8]

Therefore, the phrase "unfinished work" rings true for both Jefferson and Lincoln because neither reached closure on many of the important topics of his day. Both men understood that important ideas persist, and both expected the nation to return periodically to fundamental ideas and thereby keep them alive: ideas without closure. A corollary to this thought is that both men understood that words and the way they are presented (or, perhaps in the case of Lincoln, re-presented) matter. Although Jefferson lived a long time and engaged in many pursuits, he revisited key ideas and principles throughout his life, including the rights and responsibilities of citizenship and the proper roles of government at the local, state, and national levels, to name only two. Lincoln did not enjoy the luxury of a long life in which to develop his views fully on these and other topics, but he also found some ideas to be more important than others, including the ability of the American people to control their political destiny and how the Constitution would need to be changed as a result of the Civil War.

Friend Joshua Speed recalled that Lincoln once confided to him, "I am slow to learn, and slow to forget that which I have learned."[9]

Third, the ideas with which Jefferson and Lincoln wrestled are still integral to civic discussions, but individuals who quote their words today frequently do so without regard for the contexts in which the two men embedded them. Jefferson and Lincoln understood that they were addressing ideas fundamental to understanding not only America's history but also the continuing influence of the past on the present. In contrast, in the highly contentious society in which we live, editorialists and politicians typically mine Jefferson's and Lincoln's writings for snippets or sound bites to prop up whatever perspective on an issue they want to spin. Doing so leads to what historians refer to as "presentism," reading history backward based on our concerns, not those of past generations.

More dangerously for the survival of our democratic republic, contemporary commentators and political figures frequently diminish the importance of the ideas Jefferson and Lincoln addressed by shying away from difficult questions, preferring to apply simple answers rather than engage in reasoned judgments. The ensuing chapters investigate some of the reasoned judgments that the two men offered regarding the unfinished work of the nation.

Chapter 1 compares and contrasts the two men's views on race and slavery. Although Jefferson was a slaveholder, at various times in his life he expressed concerns about the negative effects of the institution on Virginians. In *A Summary View of the Rights of British America* (1774) and the Declaration of Independence, he blamed the English kings for pressing slavery onto the American colonies, and in *Notes on the State of Virginia* (1787), he wrote, "I tremble for my country when I reflect that God is just: that his mercy cannot continue forever."[10] Still, throughout his life, he freed only a handful of his slaves.

Lincoln wrote to correspondents and said at numerous times that he was antislavery, but his path to the Thirteenth Amendment (1865), which abolished slavery and indentured servitude in the nation, was hardly linear. Although he believed that enslaved people enjoyed unalienable rights, he also expressed doubts about extending political equality to all African Americans. When he issued the Emancipation Proclamation (1863), he emphasized that it was a wartime measure and applied only to places in rebellion.

In arriving at their views on race and slavery, both men expressed strong sentiments concerning the impact of slavery on masters as well as slaves.

In *Notes*, Jefferson worried especially that slavery turned the sons of slave-holders into tyrants, and Lincoln designed the Homestead Act primarily to provide free land to immigrants and poor settlers. For much of their lives, both men subscribed to colonization of African Americans by sending them to Africa or Central America as the best solution for slavery in the nation; however, African American participation in the war effort after 1863 marked a turning point for Lincoln. Their contributions led him to pressure members of the House of Representatives to pass the Thirteenth Amendment and set the stage for political participation for African American veterans during Reconstruction.[11]

Another issue that both men addressed concerned the role of political parties in the nation (chapter 2). Prior to the 1790s, Jefferson believed that political parties were "factions"—minority coalitions intent on advancing their own agendas, often to the detriment of the nation as a whole. Therefore, when he and James Madison created the Democratic-Republican Party, they justified their actions by convincing themselves that *their* party represented the people (majority) and that Alexander Hamilton's Federalist Party was a *minority faction* intent on British recolonization. Until the end of his life, Jefferson fretted that neo-Federalists were pursuing similarly nefarious actions.

By Lincoln's time, a strong two-party system existed in the nation. Believing that with liberty came freedom of choice, Lincoln openly identified with the Whig and, following congressional passage of the Kansas-Nebraska Act, the Republican Parties. Late in his life, however, as he pondered how to reunite the nation following the Civil War, he broke with radical members of his party over plans for Reconstruction and questioned whether his political party was becoming a *faction*, in Jefferson's understanding of that term.

A major topic of continuing debate for Americans concerns how to balance national and state powers under the Constitution (chapter 3). Jefferson believed that the Constitution bound the national government to specified powers related to the common welfare, notably foreign relations and—especially—national defense. From the 1790s onward, he read the Constitution backward from the Tenth Amendment ("powers not delegated to the United States by the Constitution, nor prohibited by it to the States, are reserved to the States respectively, or to the people"). Based on this belief, he wrote in his Kentucky Resolutions (1798) that the states had created the Constitution and therefore could collectively determine when national legislation was unconstitutional (*states' rights*).

Lincoln agreed with Jefferson's position that the Constitution created a federal republic by dividing powers between the national government and the states but accepted the "implied powers" interpretation of the Constitution (Article I, Section 8), that Congress could pass "necessary and proper" legislation to implement its specified powers. He subscribed to the idea of *state rights*, including the right of a state to determine whether to permit slavery, but he read the Constitution forward, emphasizing that the *American people*, not states, had created the document.[12]

Although Jefferson emphasized the collective right of states to rein in excessive actions of the national government, and both he and Lincoln subscribed to the theory of federalism, neither believed that a state could secede from the Union. Jefferson favored political change through frequent elections; Lincoln, through constitutional amendment.

In both Jefferson's time and Lincoln's, many Americans believed that the United States stood in a covenant relationship with God and expected the president to act according to God's will (chapter 4). Both presidents made public appeals for God's blessings on the nation, but neither subscribed to the proposition that the United States enjoyed a privileged relationship with God. Jefferson wrote approvingly in June 1824 to a correspondent who had concluded that Christian teachings were not part of the common law, calling that belief "a conspiracy between Church and State."[13] For his part, Lincoln referred to Americans in an address to the New Jersey senate in 1861 as God's "almost chosen people."[14]

In his "Bill for Establishing Religious Freedom" in Virginia (proposed in 1777, adopted in 1786), Jefferson wrote that "rulers [are] themselves but fallible and uninspired men." Therefore, he believed that for a public official to act upon his personal religious principles destroyed freedom of religion.[15] Consistent with this belief, in 1802 he pledged in a letter to the Danbury Connecticut Baptist Association that as president he would not breach the "wall of separation between church and State" erected in the First Amendment to the Constitution.[16] Before becoming president, Lincoln had not shared publicly many of his religious beliefs. During the war, he came to believe that the war happened because humans willed it but that dictating its end once it had begun was beyond human control. As the war's horrors exceeded mortal understanding, he concluded that only God could bring about an end to the fighting, and he expressed this belief in his second inaugural address.

In both eras, people wanted a president who believed he was God's agent on earth. Instead, they encountered a chief executive who believed that he had no more insight than anyone else into God's will.

Chapter 5 addresses another topic that continues to provoke controversy: the extent of the powers the president exercises under the Constitution and how Jefferson and Lincoln acted on their understanding of these powers. As president, Jefferson made war on the Barbary Coast pirates without a congressional declaration of war (1801–05); authorized purchasing the Louisiana Territory from France (1803) while believing the Constitution did not grant that power to the national government; claimed "executive privilege" to prevent his testifying in Aaron Burr's 1807 trial for treason; and expanded national authority to cover violations of the Embargo Act of 1807. Jefferson coined an important justification for his desire to acquire Louisiana when he suggested to a Kentucky senator that people of the nation would approve the expedient purchase as an "act of indemnity" (that is, an exemption from penalties attaching to unconstitutional or illegal actions granted to public officials).[17]

Lincoln also exercised powers beyond what the Constitution expressly states. He called for troops and spent money without congressional authorization; imposed a blockade on Southern ports; and denied a writ of habeas corpus to various individuals because it was a time of rebellion. In contrast to Jefferson, however, Lincoln acknowledged the supremacy of the Constitution over all his actions when he specifically asked Congress to grant retroactive ratification of his actions (i.e., acts of indemnity), which it did.

Both men also wrote about the proper role of government in promoting economic growth, because what people do for their livelihood helps define their role in society (chapter 6). For much of his life, Jefferson thought government should be active in promoting an agricultural economic system, believing that farmers controlled their lives independently of government interference. In *Notes*, he wrote, "Those who labour in the earth are the chosen people of God, if ever he had a chosen people," and he promised in his first inaugural address, "encouragement of agriculture, and of commerce as its handmaid." When the War of 1812, however, demonstrated the nation's dependence on foreign trade and inability to manufacture needed supplies, he changed his mind. In 1816, he wrote to a correspondent that manufacturing had to be placed side by side with agriculture so that the nation could preserve its independence from reliance on foreign trade.[18]

Lincoln, by way of contrast, thought government should actively invest in the nation's infrastructure. He consistently endorsed the components of Henry Clay's American System, which required national or local government to promote economic growth through a protective tariff; financial support for internal improvements (such as roads, canals, navigation of rivers and streams, and railroads); and the creation of an integrated national market. Nonetheless, at the root of Lincoln's views of the proper role of the national government in directing the nation's economy was the Jeffersonian ideal of equal economic opportunity ("all men are created equal") as the defining principle of a republic.

As a corollary to the government's proper role in guiding economic growth, both men favored public support for education. Jefferson believed that education preserved liberty. In *Notes*, he proposed universal education for Virginia's children for three years and thereafter state support for males through college on the basis of merit. In his annual message to Congress in 1806, he advocated the need for a national university, but in his retirement, he settled for founding the University of Virginia.

Although Lincoln was self-educated, he wrote in his 1832 letter introducing himself to voters as a candidate for the Illinois legislature that he viewed education "as the most important subject which we as a people can be engaged in."[19] Then, in an 1859 address to the Wisconsin State Agricultural Society, he advocated what he termed "cultivated thought" (the academic study of the sciences) in order to make communities "alike independent of crowned-kings, money-kings, and land-kings."[20] Lincoln's wishes (and perhaps, were he still alive, Jefferson's) later found congressional support in the Morrill Act (1862), which gave states public lands the sale of which provided money to create agricultural and mechanical colleges.

Finally, the epilogue probes the fact that overall Lincoln changed his ideas on key issues more than Jefferson did and seeks to explain why. Although both men drew strength from the places where they lived, for Jefferson, *place* created *a people*. At various times in his life, Jefferson expressed doubts about Virginians' behaviors, but when he traveled, he measured every place and every person against his country. He treasured his time at Monticello and, after his retirement from the presidency in 1809, his retreat, Poplar Forest.

Lincoln was born in Kentucky, moved with his family to Indiana, and as a young man settled in Illinois. Although he built a nice house for himself and his family in Springfield, for Lincoln, *people* created *the place*. As a result, he was able to redefine himself repeatedly throughout his life by identifying with different people—sequentially, the inhabitants of Sangamon County, Illinois; all Illinoisans; Republicans; Northerners; and finally, all Americans.

Jefferson and Lincoln lived during crucial times. Jefferson more than any of his contemporaries *thought* for the nation at its founding, and Lincoln *fought* to preserve the nation's founding ideas during the Civil War.[21] Although neither was able to accomplish the full measure of what he envisioned for the nation, each addressed important areas of common concern for their times and ours. Both cared deeply about the nation's republican experiment, and their words stand as touchstones for measuring our history against the promises of our beginning and as signposts for continuing their unfinished work into our future.

Chapter One

"IN *GIVING* FREEDOM TO THE *SLAVE,* WE *ASSURE* FREEDOM TO THE *FREE*"

Writer Larry L. King recalls in his 1971 autobiography, *Confessions of a White Racist,* growing up in a West Texas town and learning one day in his town's public library that George Washington and Thomas Jefferson were slaveholders. "It was shocking," King wrote, "to learn that demigods who had influenced documents affirming the thrilling, limitless doctrine that *all men are created equal* had been otherwise capable of holding men in bondage for the profit from their sweat. I well remember discovering these new lessons . . . and then standing outside [the library], looking up at the windswept streets, and thinking, 'Hell, if they lied to me about *that,* they've lied to me about everything.'"[1]

King may have dramatized his experience to a certain extent, but his realization is not uncommon to others who live in a nation born with the Enlightenment ideal of equality yet where indentured servitude and African American slavery were seen as indispensable components of the way of life in numerous localities. This situation was especially true in the American South, where the transition from indentured servitude to slavery provided increased possibilities for human exploitation.[2]

Although Thomas Jefferson grew up in this world and held slaves, he belonged to a small cadre of Virginians who believed that slavery was wrong and needed to be abolished primarily because of the negative effects it was having on the gentry-dominated society. Early in his life, Jefferson pursued attempts to remove slavery from Virginia and the nation, but he devoted less zeal to that project the older he grew. By the end of his life, he withdrew completely from efforts proposed by others to accomplish what he had advocated earlier in his life.

Abraham Lincoln was also born into a slave society (Kentucky), but he spent most of his youth in Indiana, where slavery had initially been established in the early 1800s but whose first state constitution (1816) banned the practice, and Illinois. In Illinois, slavery was initially unable to take hold because of the Northwest Ordinance of 1787, which prohibited the practice, as well as the first state constitution in 1816, but it took substantial effort in the 1820s by Governor Edward Coles to beat back attempts to write a new state constitution that would have legalized the institution (more on Coles below).

Although not intimately involved with slavery in his early life, Lincoln used the issue of expansion of slavery into territories following passage of the Kansas-Nebraska Act (1854) in a similar fashion to Jefferson by asserting the negative effects of the institution on white settlers and the threat that slavery posed to Northerners in the wake of the Supreme Court's Dred Scott decision (1857). Also like Jefferson, throughout the 1850s and into the first two years of Lincoln's presidency, he clung to hopes of African American colonization. Only as he realized that freeing slaves in areas in rebellion against the United States might aid the war effort did he commit himself to emancipation, and as a result of African American military contributions, he devoted himself wholeheartedly to the passage of the Thirteenth Amendment.

I

Jefferson's first public attack on slavery occurred in his pamphlet titled *A Summary View of the Rights of British America* (1774). Although most of Jefferson's charges of abridging the rights of the American colonists fell on Parliament (e.g., prohibiting manufacturing, restricting trade to Great Britain in British ships, and imposing duties on tea and other commodities), Jefferson blamed the English kings for prohibiting colonial legislatures from abolishing slavery and for limiting the number of slaves entering the colonies. "The abolition of domestic slavery is the great object of desire in those colonies," he asserted, "where it was unhappily introduced in their infant state." All attempts to exclude future importations of slaves, however, had been denied, and "our repeated attempts to effect this by prohibitions, and by imposing duties which might amount to a prohibition, have been hitherto defeated by his majesty's negative." From these circumstances, Jefferson concluded that the kings preferred "the immediate advantages of a few British corsairs to the lasting interests of the American states, and to the rights of human nature deeply wounded by this infamous practice."[3]

Similarly, Jefferson blamed King George III in his "Rough draught" of the Declaration of Independence for abusing the natural rights of the colonists by subjecting them to some two dozen infractions, each of which Jefferson began with the words "He has." One charge that members of the Second Continental Congress refused to adopt blamed the king for introducing and perpetuating the existence of slavery in the American colonies. In addition, Jefferson blamed the king for the actions of Royal Governor John Murray, the Earl of Dunmore, for offering freedom to slaves living in Virginia who deserted their masters and fought for the British:

> He has waged cruel war against human nature itself, violating its most sacred rights of life and liberty in the persons of a distant people who never offended him, captivating and carrying them into slavery in another hemisphere, or to incur miserable death in their transportation hither. This piratical warfare, the opprobrium of infidel powers, is the warfare of the Christian king of Great Britain. Determined to keep open a market where MEN should be bought and sold, he has prostituted his negative for suppressing every legislative attempt to prohibit or to restrain this execrable commerce. And that this assemblage of horrors might want no fact of distinguished die, he is now exciting those very people to rise in arms among us, and to purchase that liberty of which he has deprived them, by murdering the people on whom he also obtruded them: thus paying off former crimes committed against the liberties of one people, with crimes which he urges them to commit against the lives of another.[4]

If it may be said that *A Summary View* provided much of the logic and language for the Declaration, Jefferson turned the tables in June 1776. While he was at Philadelphia writing the Declaration of Independence, his gentry peers were meeting at Williamsburg to write a new state constitution. Unable to participate in the Virginia debates, Jefferson did the next best thing and sent a draft of a constitution for the state to the Constitutional Convention. Whereas the charges against the king come last in the Declaration of Independence, they are first in the Virginia Constitution of 1776 and include a pared-down version of the charge that the delegates removed from the Declaration: "by prompting our negroes to rise in arms among us; those very negroes whom he hath from time to time by an inhuman use of his negative he hath refused permission to exclude by law." Jefferson also included

Page three of Jefferson's "Rough draught" of the Declaration of Independence, where he blames the king for introducing and perpetuating slavery in the American colonies. Members of the Second Continental Congress omitted this passage from the final version of the Declaration. *Declaration of Independence, Library of Congress.*

in his draft constitution a section that would have stipulated, "No person hereafter coming into this count[r]y shall be held within the same in slavery under any pretext whatever." He included similar language in his Northwest Ordinance (1784), the legislation to organize the territories that Virginia and other states ceded to the United States: "That after the year 1800 . . . there shall be neither slavery nor involuntary servitude in any of the said states."[5]

Although unsuccessful in his attempts to influence the wording of his state's constitution, Jefferson renewed his attack on slavery in Virginia in *Notes on the State of Virginia* (1787). In Query XIV, on justice and laws, Jefferson recounted that he had introduced legislation to free slaves after a particular date and colonize them somewhere outside of Virginia "with arms, implements of household and of the handicraft arts, seeds, pairs of useful domestic animals &c. to declare them a free and independant people, and to extend to them our alliance and protection, till they have acquired strength." Colonization was necessary, Jefferson argued, because there would be too many remembrances of wrongs committed and injuries sustained to allow for peaceful coexistence. Also, he wrote, because slaves were black, mixture of a slave with his master would "[stain] the blood of his master. . . . [Therefore, w]hen freed, he is to be removed beyond the reach of mixture."[6]

These are strong words, but Jefferson raised the issue to biblical proportions in Query XVIII, on customs and manners, when he wrote, "I tremble for my country when I reflect that God is just: that his justice cannot sleep forever: that . . . a revolution of the wheel of fortune, an exchange of situation, is among possible events: that it may become probable by supernatural interference! The Almighty has no attribute which can take side with us in such a contest."[7] In this context, it is important to realize that he anticipated that his book would create controversy and therefore expressed reluctance to have it published. Writing to James Madison in May 1785 concerning possible widespread publication of his *Notes*, he begged Madison "to peruse it carefully because I ask your advice on it and ask nobody else's. . . . [T]here are sentiments on some subjects [in it] which I apprehend might be displeasing to the country perhaps to the assembly or to some who lead it."[8]

The following month, Jefferson also confided to the Frenchman François Jean de Beauvoir, Marquis de Chastellux, "The strictures on slavery and on the constitution of Virginia . . . are the parts which I do not wish to have made public, at least till I know whether their publication would do most harm or good. It is possible that in my own country these strictures might produce an irritation which would indispose the people towards the two great objects I have in view, that is the emancipation of their slaves, and the settlement of their constitution on a firmer and more permanent basis." He then added that because he thought that the book might hinder efforts to abolish slavery, he had "printed and reserved just copies enough to be able to give one to every young man at the College," saying that he "look[ed] to the rising generation, and not to the one now in power for these great reformations."[9] As this letter to Chastellux indicates, Jefferson as minister to France in the 1780s expressed embarrassment to French literati who challenged the author of the Declaration of Independence on the fact that slavery was antithetical to the document's ringing endorsement of the doctrine of "unalienable rights."

As president, Jefferson supported Virginia's 1802 plan to allow individual masters to free their slaves as long as they removed them from the state, and he initially favored colonization for free blacks, probably in Sierra Leone. As Douglas Egerton has so masterfully demonstrated, however, between 1802 and 1805, Jefferson's ardor for such a plan cooled, perhaps in part due to fears that Toussaint Louverture's slave rebellion in French-controlled Saint Domingue would inspire similar efforts among enslaved people in Virginia. President Jefferson pursued a policy of diplomatic isolation for the island, he lent his support to a total ban on trade with the rebels in 1805, and the Embargo Act of 1807 sealed the fate of the former slave leadership on the island. Normal diplomatic relations between the now independent country of Haiti and the United States did not return until 1862, during Abraham Lincoln's presidency.[10]

Following his retirement from the presidency, Jefferson withdrew even further from pursuing any active interest in issues like ending slavery in Virginia. Not even a letter from Edward Coles, James Madison's personal secretary, in August 1814 specifically asking Jefferson to take up the challenge once again to try to abolish slavery could move him to action. Coles was born near Charlottesville but was forty-three years younger than Jefferson. Like Jefferson, Coles had attended the College of William and Mary, where, as a student, he determined to free his slaves at some point in his life. In 1814, when he wrote to Jefferson, Coles was moving to act on his earlier resolve and wrote to Jefferson to enlist the elder man's aid in the task of promoting legislation for that purpose.

Jefferson demurred. He had hoped that the ideals of the Revolutionary War, he wrote to Coles, would overcome slave owners' attitudes that slavery was a natural and necessary component of their lives. "Nursed and educated in the daily habit of seeing the degraded condition, both bodily and mental, of those unfortunate beings, not reflecting that that degradation was very much the work of themselves & their fathers, few minds have yet doubted but that they were as legitimate subjects of property as their horses and cattle." Therefore, he told Coles, when Richard Bland introduced legislation to move Virginia toward ending slavery, Jefferson had supported the legislation. Unfortunately, instead of moving the assembly to act on the proposal, Bland's motion caused him to be "denounced as an enemy of his country, & [be] treated with the grossest indecorum." Following this incident, Jefferson said, "other & more distant duties were assigned to me, so that from that time till my return from Europe in 1789, and I may say till I returned to reside at home in 1809, I had little opportunity of knowing the progress of public sentiment here on this subject."[11]

Although he had hoped that younger generations would take up this cause, Jefferson expressed disappointment to Coles that his was a "solitary but welcome voice," saying, "I have considered the general silence which prevails on this subject as indicating an apathy unfavorable to every hope." Jefferson vowed, therefore, to play no further role in such efforts. "I have overlived the generation with which mutual labors & perils begat mutual confidence and influence," he wrote. "This enterprise is for the young; for those who can follow it up, and bear it through to its consummation. It shall have all my prayers, & these are the only weapons of an old man."[12]

In closing, Jefferson offered the young man some advice. Since Virginia laws prohibited freeing slaves unless they were at the same time transported out of state, Jefferson urged Coles, "[R]econcile yourself to your country and its unfortunate condition; that you will not lessen its stock of sound disposition by withdrawing your portion from the mass. . . . [A]ssociate others in your labors, and when the phalanx is formed, bring on and press the proposition perseveringly until its accomplishment." In the meantime, Jefferson encouraged Coles to "be supported by the religious precept, 'be not weary in well-doing.'"[13]

Although seemingly aiming his advice at Coles, Jefferson's biblical reference was primarily self-reflexive, as indicated by his prior admission that he had already given up on any hope of success for ending slavery in Virginia. In other words, by 1814, Jefferson had himself become "weary in well-doing." As for Coles, he did not follow Jefferson's guidance. In 1820, he left Virginia with his family and property and moved to Illinois, where he freed his ten slaves. Two years later, he was elected governor of the state on an antislavery ticket and successfully defeated efforts to amend the Illinois Constitution to permit slaveholding there. In 1833, he moved to Philadelphia, where he joined with antislavery friends to work to end slavery in the nation.[14]

Two years after receiving Coles's letter, Jefferson heard from another antislavery proponent, Samuel Kercheval, that plans were being hatched to write a new constitution for Virginia that would provide for the end of slavery. Like Coles, Kercheval invited Jefferson's involvement. As with his response to Coles, however, Jefferson was unmoved to participate. "I am now retired," he wrote. "I resign myself, as a passenger, with confidence to those at present at the helm, and ask but for rest, peace and good will."[15]

The full measure of Jefferson's withdrawal from the issue may be found in two additional letters from the 1820s. The first was to Massachusetts congressman John Holmes, who represented the province of Maine during discussions leading to the Missouri Compromise, the legislation that brought Maine and Missouri into the Union—one free and the other a slave state—and prohibited slavery in the lands of the Louisiana Purchase north of the southern boundary of Missouri. Likening the Missouri question to "a fire-bell in the night," Jefferson said, "there is not a man on earth who would sacrifice more than I would to relieve us from this heavy reproach [slavery] in any *practicable* way," but doing so would have to involve "a general emancipation and *expatriation*." Someday, he wrote to Holmes, those events might be accomplished. "But as it is, we have the wolf by the [ear], and we can neither hold him, nor safely let him go. Justice is in one scale, and self-preservation in the other."[16]

The second revealing letter was to Jefferson's favorite granddaughter. In May 1825, Ellen Randolph married a Boston man, Joseph Coolidge, in the parlor at Monticello. The couple traveled through upstate New York and New England in August, and Mrs. Coolidge drew a comparison between what she observed there and life in the South. She saw, she wrote to Jefferson, "prosperity and improvement, such as I fear our Southern States cannot hope for, whilst the canker of slavery eats into their hearts, and diseases the whole body by this ulcer to the core." Reminiscent of early Virginia historians and her grandfather's own positive feelings about the climate of the Old Dominion (see the epilogue), she offered this opinion: "When I consider the immense advantages of soil and climate which we possess over these people, it grieves me to think that such great gifts of Nature should have failed to produce any thing like the wealth and improvement which the New-Englanders have wrung from the hard bosom of a stubborn and ungrateful land, and amid the gloom and desolation of their wintry skies." She closed her letter with a comparison of the people of the two regions:

"The appearance of the people generally is much in their favor; the men seem sober, orderly, and industrious: I have seen but one drunken man since I entered New England, and he was a south carolinian!" Jefferson's response was terse and defensive: "I have no doubt you will find . . . the state of society there more congenial with your mind than the rustic scenes you have left. . . . One fatal stain [i.e., slavery] deforms what nature had bestowed on us of her fairest gifts."[17]

II

Lincoln's earliest thoughts on slavery are inextricably connected with the issue of whether it should be allowed to expand beyond the limits established with the Missouri Compromise and his political admiration of Kentucky senator Henry Clay, whom Lincoln called "my beau ideal of a statesman." In October 1845, Lincoln wrote to an abolitionist concerning the issue of the annexation of Texas and his belief that Liberty Party members should have supported Clay in 1844 for president if they had been truly dedicated to stopping slavery's expansion. In Lincoln's mind, Liberty Party supporters had failed to support Clay because he was a slaveholder, but their actions had only succeeded in helping another slaveholder, Democrat James K. Polk, become president. "If by your votes you could have prevented the *extention*, &c. of slavery," Lincoln wrote, "would it not have been *good* and not *evil* so to have used your votes, even though it involved the casting of them for a slaveholder?" Lincoln then shared his personal views by saying, "I hold it to be a paramount duty of us in the free states, due to the Union of the states, and perhaps to liberty itself (paradox though it may seem) to let the slavery of the other states alone; while, on the other hand, I hold it to be equally clear, that we should never knowingly lend ourselves directly or indirectly, to prevent that slavery from dying a natural death—to find new places for it to live in, when it can no longer exist in the old."[18]

A speaking engagement at Worcester, Massachusetts, in September 1848 provided Lincoln the opportunity not only to stump for Whig presidential candidate Zachary Taylor but also to emphasize the importance for Northerners of preventing the expansion of slavery. "[T]he people of Illinois agreed entirely with the people of Massachusetts on this subject," he said, "except perhaps that they did not keep so constantly thinking about it. All agreed that slavery was an evil, but that we were not responsible for it and cannot affect it in States of this Union where we do not live. But, the question of the *extension* of slavery to new territories of this country, is a part of our responsibility and care, and is under our control."[19]

Clay's death in July 1852 gave Lincoln a platform from which to encapsulate the views that informed his actions until his issuance of the Emancipation Proclamation a decade later. At the close of his eulogy to Clay, Lincoln repeated his opposition to slavery's spread into new areas, distanced himself from abolitionists, condemned Southerners who were twisting American history to support their extreme views, and recorded his support for colonization of African Americans abroad. Lincoln portrayed Clay as a slaveholder who favored the gradual extinction of the institution in the nation. "Cast into life where slavery was already widely spread and deeply seated," Lincoln said, "he did not perceive . . . how it could at *once* be eradicated, without producing a greater evil, even to the cause of human liberty itself." In castigating abolitionists, Lincoln warned that they were willing to "shiver into fragments the Union of these States; tear to tatters its now venerated constitution; and even burn the last copy of the Bible, rather than slavery should continue a single hour." As for the few but "increasing number of men" devoted to perpetuating and expanding the scope of slavery, Lincoln called them to task for "beginning to assail and to ridicule the white-man's charter of freedom—the declaration that 'all men are created free and equal.'"[20] Regarding Clay's role in supporting the American Colonization Society from an early date, Lincoln expressed his belief that removal of African Americans to Africa would "succeed in freeing our land from the dangerous presence of slavery; and, at the same time, in restoring a captive people to their long-lost father-land, with bright prospects for the future."[21]

When the US Congress passed the Kansas-Nebraska Act in 1854, Lincoln knew exactly how to respond. Speaking at Peoria, Illinois, in October 1854, he declared that the purpose of the act was larger than simply whether slavery should be allowed in the Kansas and Nebraska territories. The net effect of the legislation, according to Lincoln, was "to spread [slavery] to every other part of the wide world, where men can be found inclined to take it." In Lincoln's mind prior to 1854, slavery had been tolerated based on necessity, but the nation's founders had placed it on the road to extinction; however, "NOW [slavery] is to be transformed into a 'sacred right'" based on self-interest. "Nebraska brings it forth, places it on the high road to extension and perpetuity; and, with a pat on its back, says to it, 'Go, and God speed you.' Henceforth it is to be the chief jewel of the nation—the very figure-head of the ship of State."[22]

In an attempt to broaden the issue further beyond Kansas and Nebraska, Lincoln argued that the territories belonged to all the people of the nation, and because of this fact, not only potential settlers in the areas but "[t]he whole nation is interested that the best use shall be made of these territories. We want them for the homes of free white people. This they cannot be, to any considerable extent, if slavery shall be planted within them. Slave States are places for poor white people to remove FROM; not to remove TO. New free States are the places for people to go to and better their condition. For this use, the nation needs these territories."[23] He repeated and emphasized this point in his last debate with Stephen Douglas in October 1858:

> Now irrespective of the moral aspect of this question as to whether there is a right or wrong in enslaving a negro, I am still in favor of our new Territories being in such a condition that white men may find a home—may find some spot where they can better their condition—where they can settle upon new soil and better their condition in life. I am in favor of this not merely . . . for our own people who are born amongst us, but as an outlet for *free white people everywhere*, the world over—in which Hans and Baptiste and Patrick, and all other men from all the world, may find new homes and better their conditions in life.[24]

As part of his argument that slaveholders were using the Kansas-Nebraska Act to increase their power in the nation, Lincoln reminded his audience that under the US Constitution, slave states enjoyed a political advantage over nonslave states because slaves increased the number of inhabitants of the states by three-fifths. Because this arrangement already existed, the matter was settled for the current states in the Union, Lincoln argued, but not for future states that might join. In his reckoning, if slave owners were able to establish slavery in Nebraska, it gave them more rights than others enjoyed and excluded these rights to other whites, thereby reducing nonslaveholders "to a still smaller fraction of a man" than already existed. Were that to occur, Lincoln taunted the members of his audience, "I should like for some gentleman deeply skilled in the mysteries of sacred rights, to provide himself with a microscope, and peep about, and find out, if he can, what has become of my sacred rights! They will surely be too small for detection with the naked eye." Put succinctly, Lincoln argued that the *right* of a slaveholder to take slaves into territories diminished the *rights* of nonslaveholders to prevent the existence of slavery in those areas.[25]

Expanding on this theme, Lincoln said that the Kansas-Nebraska Act was antithetical to the spirit of the Declaration of Independence because slavery destroyed liberty. "When the white man governs himself that is self-government; but when he governs himself, and also governs *another* man, that is *more* than self-government—that is despotism. If the negro is a *man*, why then my ancient faith teaches me that 'all men are created equal;' and that there can be no moral right in connection with one man's making a slave of another."[26]

Lincoln repeated the accusation that the Kansas-Nebraska Act violated the principles embedded in the Declaration of Independence in a letter in mid-August 1855, writing, "When we were the political slaves of King George, and wanted to be free, we called the maxim that 'all men are created equal' a self evident truth; but now when we have grown fat, and have lost all dread of being slaves ourselves, we have become so greedy as to be *masters* that we call the same maxim 'a self-evident lie.'" Similarly in a letter written that same month to his Springfield friend Joshua F. Speed, who now lived in Kentucky, Lincoln accused moderate Southerners of allowing "a small, odious and detested class" of "slave-holders and slave-traders" to "dictate the course of all of you, and are as completely your masters, as you are the masters of your own negroes."[27]

Therefore, by the time the Supreme Court ruled in *Dred Scott v. Sandford* (60 US 393 [1857]) that the Missouri Compromise was unconstitutional because it violated the Fifth Amendment guarantee to property, Lincoln had already developed his rationale with which to counter the court's ruling. At Springfield, Illinois, on June 16, 1858, Lincoln gave what later came to be known as his "House Divided" speech, in which he made public his speculation that the nation could not remain forever half slave and half free: "I do not expect the Union to be *dissolved* . . . but I *do* expect it will cease to be divided. It will become *all* one thing, or *all* the other." Lincoln found especially troublesome the fact that the Supreme Court, in denying the right of the people of a *territory* to exclude slavery, left open the possibility that the people of a *state* might soon find themselves in a similar situation: "Put *that* and *that* together, and we . . . may, ere long, see filled with another Supreme Court decision, declaring that the Constitution of the United States does not permit a *state* to exclude slavery from its limits."[28]

As he emerged as a potential Republican candidate for president, he continued to emphasize the nationalizing potential of the Dred Scott decision. For example, in his speech at Cooper Institute in February 1860, he said, "I am also aware [the Supreme Court has] not, as yet, in terms, demanded the overthrow of our Free-State Constitutions. Yet those Constitutions declare the wrong of slavery, with more solemn emphasis, than do all other sayings against it; and when all these other sayings shall have been silenced, the overthrow of these Constitutions will be demanded, and nothing be left to resist the demand." Following this important speech, he undertook a speaking tour of the New England states, and at Hartford, Connecticut, in early March he warned, "They do not ask us to change our free State constitutions, but they will yet do that. After demanding *what* they do, and *as* they do, they cannot stop short of this."[29]

In summary, as he prepared for the seven debates with Stephen Douglas, the author of the Kansas-Nebraska Act, in the summer and fall of 1858, Lincoln had established several positions, all of which connected with an opposition to the expansion of slavery beyond where it already existed. He believed that the expansion of slavery into new areas would extend Southerners' political power in the nation based on the three-fifths clause in the Constitution; territories existed as safety valves for poor, white settlers; Southern extremists, supported by the Supreme Court in the Dred Scott decision, were putting their self-interest ahead of the national interest and threatening to take slavery everywhere in the nation; and slavery was antithetical to the principles enunciated in the Declaration of Independence.

Douglas's approach during their joint appearances was to emphasize that the issue of slavery's expansion would be determined by the people who were most invested in it—settlers in the territories—and to portray Lincoln as an abolitionist and racial amalgamator who was intent on extending the rights of citizenship to African Americans and making them the equal of whites. In the first debate, for example, Douglas said, "I believe this government was made on the white basis. I believe it was made by white men, for the benefit of white men and their posterity for ever, and I am in favor of confining citizenship to white men."[30] This strategy potentially placed Lincoln in the difficult position of walking a fine line between saving the territories for whites and appearing to be an abolitionist.

Lincoln was able to defuse this strategy successfully by expanding his initial appeal to poor whites in rural areas to include urban dwellers in the North (especially immigrants) who believed that the nation was born according to principles of self-improvement. On this basis, Lincoln could even tolerate the political risk this new argument entailed by simultaneously reaching out to abolitionists by asserting that slavery elevated one group over another in the name of mere self-interest. He did this by expanding connections between Kansas-Nebraska and the Declaration of Independence instead of curtailing them. For example, in the seventh debate with Douglas, Lincoln characterized the conflict between freedom and slavery in the 1850s as

> the eternal struggle between . . . right and wrong . . . the two principles that have stood face to face from the beginning of time; and will ever continue to struggle. The one is the common right of humanity and the other the divine right of kings. . . . It is the same spirit that says, "You work and toil and earn bread, and I'll eat it." No matter in what shape it comes, whether from the mouth of a king who seeks to bestride the people of his own nation and live by the fruit of their labor, or from one race of men as an apology for enslaving another race, it is the same tyrannical principle.[31]

Lincoln was also able to counter successfully Douglas's strategy of portraying him as desiring political and social equality for blacks by saying repeatedly that "a physical difference" existed between the two races that "will probably forever forbid their living together upon the footing of perfect equality, and inasmuch as it becomes a necessity that there must be a difference, I, as well as Judge Douglas, am in favor of the race to which I belong, having the superior position." This reality notwithstanding, Lincoln said in the first debate:

> [T]here is no reason in the world why the negro is not entitled to all the natural rights enumerated in the Declaration of Independence, the right to life, liberty and the pursuit of happiness. I hold that he is as much entitled to these as the white man. I agree with Judge Douglas he is not my equal in many respects—certainly not in color, perhaps not in moral or intellectual endowment. But in the right to eat the bread, without leave of anybody else, which his own hand earns, *he is my equal and the equal of Judge Douglas, and the equal of every living man.*

When Douglas persisted in the argument that the statement of equality among men in the Declaration did not extend to African Americans, Lincoln countered in the seventh debate that the authors of that document "did not mean to assert the obvious untruth, that all were then actually enjoying that equality, nor yet, that they were about to confer it immediately upon them. . . . They meant simply to declare the *right* so that the *enforcement* of it might follow as fast as circumstances should permit."[32]

Because of his belief in state rights (see chapter 3) and his strong opposition to the expansion of slavery, Lincoln moved slowly as president to end the institution. In the eulogy that he offered at the time of Henry Clay's death, Lincoln indicated that he, like Clay, favored colonization as the preferred way to address the issue of slavery in the nation. "If as the friends of colonization hope," he said, "the present and coming generations of our countrymen shall by any means, succeed in freeing our land from the dangerous presence of slavery; and at the same time, in restoring a captive people to their long-lost father-land, with bright prospects for the future; and this too, by the change, it will indeed be a glorious consummation."

During the first two years of his administration, he continued to pursue plans for colonizing African Americans and preserving western territories for white settlers. For example, in his annual message in December 1861, he united the two initiatives by asking Congress to appropriate money for finding a suitable place for African Americans to settle, "for the emigration of colored men leaves additional room for white men remaining or coming here."[33] Passage of the Homestead Act in mid-1862 fulfilled part of this goal. This historic piece of legislation cannot be divorced from the context of the Civil War, as Lincoln and Congress wanted to ensure that the territories in the West would be settled by people who supported the Union, especially if a reconciliation between North and South was to occur, but its justification resided in Lincoln's thinking that had evolved over the preceding decade. In opening about 10 percent of the nation's lands to settlement, the president made good on his statements from 1854 onward that slavery should be excluded from the territories and that these lands should be settled by people who wanted to advance their condition. After the war, former slaves took advantage of the legislation, but the majority of the settlers were poor whites, including recent immigrants and single women.

Also, just before issuing the Emancipation Proclamation, Lincoln met on August 13, 1862, at the White House with a group of prominent African Americans. He told them that they should become leaders in creating a colony for blacks in Central America so that they could have a place where they could advance themselves. "You and we are different races," he said.

"We have between us a broader difference than exists between almost any other two races. Whether it is right or wrong I need not discuss, but this physical difference is a great disadvantage to us both. . . . I cannot alter it if I would. It is a fact, about which we all think and feel alike."³⁴

Despite these statements, Lincoln's thinking about slavery—especially as it connected to the war effort to suppress the rebellion—was changing by the summer of 1862. In a now famous public letter to Horace Greeley, editor of the *New York Tribune*, Lincoln affirmed that ending slavery was not his "paramount object" in the war. "What I do about slavery, and the colored race, I do because I believe it helps to save the Union; and what I forbear, I forbear because I do *not* believe it would help to save the Union. I shall do *less* whenever I shall believe what I am doing hurts the cause, and I shall do *more* whenever I shall believe doing more will help the cause."³⁵ One week before issuing the preliminary Emancipation Proclamation, Lincoln told a group of Chicago ministers that he viewed emancipation from the perspective of whether it would advance suppressing the rebellion. "I admit," he said, "that slavery is the root of the rebellion, or at least its *sine qua non*. The ambition of politicians may have instigated them to act, but they would have been impotent without slavery as their instrument. . . . I have not decided against a proclamation of liberty to the slaves, but hold the matter under advisement. And I can assure you that the subject is on my mind, by day and night, more than any other."³⁶

Given all that he had written and said prior to the Emancipation Proclamation, the announcement on September 22, 1862, marked a major turning point for Lincoln. Born out of military necessity and framed in such a way as to offer freedom to slaves in rebel areas but not in the border states, Lincoln's order, as implemented on January 1, 1863, welcomed African Americans into service in the US military, albeit in segregated units. In his meeting with the Chicago ministers, he had expressed the fear that if African American troops were armed, they would desert, and the arms "would be in the hands of the rebels; and indeed thus far we have not had arms enough to equip our white troops." The final Emancipation Proclamation indicates that he was willing to set aside these doubts.³⁷

An even more dramatic example of the magnitude of Lincoln's change of thinking may be seen by comparing his 1861 annual message to Congress with that of the following year. Although in the latter document, he wrote, "I cannot make it better known than it already is, that I strongly favor colonization," he followed that statement with this one: "[T]here is an objection urged against free colored persons remaining in the country, which is largely imaginary, if not sometimes malicious." Even though he proposed that Congress appropriate funds to compensate slave owners for freeing their slaves, the context for this proposal was radically different than previously. "In *giving* freedom to the *slave*, we *assure* freedom to the *free*— honorable alike in what we give, and what we preserve. We shall nobly save, or meanly lose, the last best, hope of earth." He also said in that speech that nothing Congress might do would affect his Emancipation Proclamation, which was scheduled to take effect on January 1, 1863.[38]

As historian Eric Foner demonstrates so convincingly, over time African American soldiers' devotion to the cause caused Lincoln to reverse his previously expressed views on their suitability for military service.[39] On July 30, 1863, Lincoln issued an Order of Retaliation, which declared, "It is the duty of every government to give protection to its citizens, of whatever class, color, or condition, and especially to those who are duly organized as soldiers in the public service.... The government of the United States will give the same protection to all its soldiers, and if the enemy shall sell or enslave anyone because of his color, the offense shall be punished by retaliation upon the enemy's prisoners in our possession."[40] The full measure of Lincoln's commitment to the proclamation and to the African Americans who answered the call is evident in his 1863 annual message to Congress. There had been numerous attempts, he wrote, to have him rescind his proclamation or lessen the strength of the measures to put it into effect, but he pledged not to do so. "To now abandon [those who had responded to the proclamation] would be not only to relinquish a lever of power, but would also be a cruel and an astounding breach of faith. I may add at this point, that while I remain in my present position I shall not attempt to retract or modify the emancipation proclamation; nor shall I return to slavery any person who is free by the terms of that proclamation, or by any acts of Congress."[41]

Finally, Lincoln's commitment to fundamental change that the Emancipation Proclamation produced may be seen by looking closely at the text of the Gettysburg Address. "Equality of condition" is one of its major themes. Ten days before he took the oath of office and became the sixteenth president of the United States, Lincoln gave a speech in Independence Hall at Philadelphia, in which he said that he "never had a feeling politically that did not spring from the sentiments embodied in the Declaration of

Independence. . . . It was that which gave promise that in due time the weights should be lifted from the shoulders of all men, and that *all* should have an equal chance. This is the sentiment embodied in that Declaration of Independence."[42] As Garry Wills argues so persuasively, Lincoln used his small spotlight at the dedication of the cemetery in 1863 to return the nation to the principles of the Declaration of Independence.[43] And for the nation to embrace once again the proposition that "all men are created equal," the Constitution would have to be changed. At the end of his two-minute speech, Lincoln said that the soldiers who died at Gettysburg had given "the last full measure of [their] devotion" so that the United States "shall have *a new birth of freedom*."[44]

He followed through with the necessity to amend the Constitution in order to eliminate slavery in anticipation of the presidential election of 1864. In reply to a committee notifying him of his renomination in early June 1864, Lincoln wrote that he would wait to accept the honor until he read the party's platform to confirm that it included ratification of the Thirteenth Amendment. "[S]uch [an] amendment to the Constitution . . . [is] a fitting, and necessary conclusion to the final success of the Union cause. Such alone can meet and cover all cavils. . . . In the joint names of Liberty and Union, let us labor to give it legal form, and practical effect."[45] Therefore, when the House of Representatives passed the resolution approving the Thirteenth Amendment on February 1, 1865, Lincoln signed the resolution even though presidents have no say in whether constitutional amendments will become the law of the land. The editor of *The Collected Works of Abraham Lincoln* says that he "signed in accordance with his usual practice of approving resolutions and acts of congress,"[46] but Lincoln's own words belie this. In response to a serenade in the evening of the House's action, Lincoln proclaimed the amendment as "a King's cure for all . . . evils. It winds the whole thing up. He would repeat that it was the fitting if not indispensable adjunct to the consummation of the great game we are playing. He could not but congratulate all present, himself, the country and the whole world upon this great moral victory."[47]

Although it is impossible to know for sure what Lincoln meant by saying that the Thirteenth Amendment was "a King's cure" for the evils of slavery, it may be said that by the time he gave his last public speech on April 11, 1865, he was moving beyond the Declaration's "unalienable rights" of life, liberty, and the pursuit of happiness to include political equality for "very intelligent" blacks and "those who serve our cause as soldiers." Speaking within the context of Reconstruction efforts to allow the state of Louisiana to rejoin the United States, Lincoln encouraged Congress to support a plan whereby whites and blacks would work together to advance their state and the nation: "The colored man . . . in seeing all united for him, is inspired with vigilance, and energy, and daring, to the same end. Grant that he desires the elective franchise, will he not attain it sooner by saving the already advanced steps toward it, than by running backward over them? . . . [And] if we reject Louisiana, we also reject one vote in favor of the proposed [Thirteenth] amendment to the national constitution."[48]

III

At the start of his political career, Thomas Jefferson wrote attacks on slavery and proposed in his draft constitution for the state that Virginia abolish the practice, but his zeal for changing his countrymen's behaviors diminished with the end of the Revolutionary War. Pushing this issue would certainly have led to his ostracism from society, because the great majority of Jefferson's peers had no inclination to alter the economic underpinning of their lives so radically. Although he saw clearly what needed to be done to impart justice to slaves and improve the work ethic of the gentry class in Virginia, he bent to their wishes when confronted by opposition.

In trying to understand why Jefferson did not advocate the issue of slavery's abolition more forcefully, the explanation that seems to be the most salient is that he never developed a steady commitment based on doubts he entertained about African American equality. In this regard, his views on slavery were conventional rather than exceptional. He believed—as did his society at large, down, in fact, to Lincoln's time—that African Americans were "inferior to the whites in the endowments of both body and mind. . . . [The] unfortunate difference of colour, and perhaps of faculty, is a powerful obstacle to the emancipation of these people."[49] During his life and in his will, he freed only those slaves who were part of the Hemings family, some of whom were likely his children.

Because he could not accept equality between masters and slaves, Jefferson's reasons for wanting to end slavery centered primarily on the negative effects he believed the institution was having on the master class, especially their children. Reliance on the labor of others, in Jefferson's mind, was an easy but essentially self-destructive behavior. Placing his hopes in the younger generation—especially that they would recognize the error of their ways and change—proved to be especially misguided, as the youths, with the notable exception of Edward Coles, demonstrated no more interest in ending the institution than had their ancestors.

Abraham Lincoln grew to adulthood sharing many of Jefferson's beliefs about African American inferiority, but in contrast to Jefferson, he believed that the right to advance oneself economically extended to all male Americans. Therefore, although he was slow to recognize the full impact of the revolutionary nature of his thinking, Lincoln eventually changed his perspective and took the nation in a new direction based on the contribution African American soldiers made to the war effort.

In his recent book, historian David Williams recounts a conversation between a Republican politician in Illinois after the war and Duncan Winslow, a former slave and Union veteran. In asking for Winslow's support in an upcoming election, the candidate said, "Don't forget. We freed you people." In response, Winslow raised his wounded arm and said, "See this? Looks to me like I freed myself."[50] One wonders what Lincoln would have thought if he had lived long enough to learn of this exchange.

"YOU ENQUIRE WHERE I NOW STAND"

The United States since the end of George Washington's first administration has been governed by one of two political parties. In the early 1790s, Alexander Hamilton created a political party in order to advance his economic and foreign policy agendas, and Thomas Jefferson and his friend James Madison created an opposition political party to counter him. The party Jefferson and Madison organized won control of the presidency in the election of 1800, and the transfer of power that occurred following that election set the precedence for two-party rule in the nation, based on plebiscite.

Jefferson rationalized the necessity of his party to save the nation from Federalist attempts to undermine the Constitution by reestablishing monarchical rule. Jefferson viewed his election as preserving the twin principles for which the American Revolution had been fought: federalism, the division of powers between the national and state governments, and republicanism, popular control of the government. After the War of 1812, he celebrated the fact that it had led to the demise of the Federalist Party but lamented the existence of neo-Federalists, who, in his view, persisted in attempts to subvert federalism and republicanism.

By way of contrast, Abraham Lincoln came of age in an era when competition between two national parties had become an accepted part of American pluralism. As a result, at the start of his political career, Lincoln joined the Whig Party because it reflected his views of what was best for the nation. With the demise of the Whigs in the aftermath of the Kansas-Nebraska Act (1854), he became a standard-bearer of the Republican Party and its presidential candidate in the election of 1860 because he believed only this party could save the nation from dismemberment, a position that he espoused throughout his presidency. Near the end of his life, however, as Lincoln began to question the wisdom of radical members of his party based on his dedication to reconcile North and South following the Civil War, he also began to doubt the wisdom of party allegiance.

Although Americans have over time embraced the existence of two dominant political parties, they continue to harbor suspicions that "party unity" may not always align totally with the welfare of the nation as a whole. Studying Jefferson's and Lincoln's views on political parties not only promotes an examination of the origins of the nation's two-party system but also provides a vantage point from which to reflect on the purpose of parties under the Constitution, which nowhere mentions them as entities.

I

Many Americans are surprised to learn that political parties are not mentioned in the US Constitution. In fact, the men who met in Philadelphia in the summer of 1787 to hammer out the document that has governed the operation of politics in the nation for more than two hundred years subscribed to English traditions that equated notions of political party with the word *faction*, a small group of people bound together by common interests who worked for narrow gains for themselves, often by subverting the general will of the people. In England, both Whigs, who were supporters of the House of Commons in the Parliament, and Tories, the king's supporters, purported to work for national unity, and members of each group viewed their opponents—but not themselves—as affiliates of a faction.[1]

Not surprisingly, these views were transferred to the new nation, but partisan divisions quickly became a fact of life at both local and national levels. Divisions between small and large states at the Constitutional Convention threatened to destroy the compromises necessary to complete the document, and sides formed following the convention, with the Federalists calling for adoption of the new form of government, and the Antifederalists wanting to reject the text and continue under the country's original form of government, the Articles of Confederation.

Federalists argued that the Constitution continued the American Revolution because the American people had declared their independence as a unit based on the principle that constitutional change was the responsibility of the people of the United States. States, which were sovereign entities under the Articles of Confederation, were never separate from the nation and therefore were never sovereign prior to the existence of the articles (1781). They further contended that under the articles, the jealousies and selfish interests of states were destroying national cohesiveness, and they believed that these narrow perspectives were threatening the existence of the nation. For Federalists, the nation had reached a time of crisis; it was possible to save either the articles or the nation, but not both.

Antifederalists countered these arguments with the assertion that the states defended the liberties of Americans under the Declaration of Independence and that the Constitution would dissolve local autonomy. They further contended that only a government that remained locally based ensured the right of the people to check the actions of their representatives and that the existence of a national capital would create a new breed of aristocrats, all safely out of reach of the people.

Because he was US minister to France when the Constitutional Convention met and did not return to the United States until after George Washington had been elected president, Jefferson was not immediately swept up in the contentious debates over whether the people, meeting in their states, should ratify the Constitution. As he prepared to return in March 1789, Jefferson wrote to Francis Hopkinson to clarify his views on the partisan division between Federalists and Antifederalists. In this letter, Jefferson said that his views did not align perfectly with those of either group; rather, he preferred to be independent of both. "I never submitted the whole system of my opinions," he wrote, "to the creed of any party of men whatever in religion, in philosophy, in politics, or in any thing else where I was capable of thinking for myself. Such an addition is the last degradation of a free and moral agent. If I could not go to heaven but with a party, I would not go there at all." He then reiterated his views on the positives and negatives in the Constitution (discussed below) and concluded, "[B]y [these] you will see that I am of neither party, nor yet a trimmer between parties."[2]

Jefferson's letter alludes to the fact that a lively newspaper warfare had developed in the nation to advance the arguments on whether to adopt the Constitution, especially in the key state of New York, where Alexander Hamilton, James Madison, and John Jay wrote under the pen name "Publius" to present the pro side of the argument. These essays, later published collectively as *The Federalist Papers*, assured New Yorkers that the Constitution was necessary to save the nation from financial and international disaster, while also arguing that this document—and not the Articles of Confederation—continued the ideals of the American Revolution.

Nonetheless, in his essays, Hamilton clearly favored making the powers of the national government stronger than state authority in order to bind the nation more closely together than had been the case under the articles. For example, in "Federalist #15," Hamilton wrote, "The measures of the Union have not been executed; and the delinquencies of the States have step by step matured themselves to an extreme, which has, at length, arrested all the wheels of the national government and brought them to an awful stand." Later, in "Federalist #23," he tipped his hand even further when he wrote that the nation needed a constitution "at least equally energetic with the one proposed" in order to preserve the nation. In other words, Hamilton was skeptical that the Constitution was strong enough to bind the states into an enduring union, and he later designed his political program as treasury secretary with this purpose in mind.[3]

Although James Madison in the 1790s disagreed strongly with Hamilton about the powers that the national government legitimately enjoyed under the Constitution, Madison's Federalist essays also downplayed the fact that the document dramatically increased the powers of the national government at the expense of the states. In "Federalist #39," for example, Madison characterized the document as "in strictness, neither a national nor a federal Constitution, but a composition of both. In its foundation it is federal, not national; in the sources from which the ordinary powers of the government are drawn, it is partly federal and partly national; in the operation of these powers, it is national, not federal; in the extent of them, again, it is federal, not national; and, finally, in the authoritative mode of introducing amendments, it is neither wholly federal nor wholly national."[4]

Madison extended the idea that the Constitution was designed to harmonize the interests of the national and state governments with the reasoning in "Federalist #51" that the Constitution had accorded each entity specific and distinctive responsibilities. "In the compound republic of America," he wrote, "the power surrendered by the people is first divided between two distinct governments, and then the portion allotted to each subdivided among distinct and separate departments. Hence a double security arises to the rights of the people. The different governments will control each other, at the same time that each will be controlled by itself." In other words, by limiting the national and state governments to specified powers and by separating the powers among legislative, executive, and judicial authority, the American people bound government to act responsibly. One further safeguard to the people's liberties embodied in the Constitution, Madison argued in "Federalist #10," involved creating a large republic, by which factions would be spread out and thereby be less likely to join together to form a tyrannical majority ruling group.[5]

Some of the divisions between Federalists and Antifederalists persisted beyond the ratification debates in the states during 1787–88, but differences of opinion in the first Congress concerning Alexander Hamilton's financial plan and foreign policy initiatives spawned new voting blocs either supporting Hamilton's program or opposing it. Eventually, these rifts produced political battles between the Federalists, the name Hamilton and his backers chose in order to attach themselves to the initial battle over ratification, and Hamilton's detractors.

Hamilton continued to refer to those who supported his financial program, which included assuming state and national debts from the American Revolution at face value, implementing a protective tariff, creating a national bank, and establishing an excise tax on whiskey, as Federalists in order to make the case that the national government was simply implementing prior, agreed-upon arrangements. He emphasized especially that he and his supporters sought to promote national unity by binding the states and individual Americans to the power and authority of the national government, thereby lessening local attachments to states.

Madison and Jefferson opposed Hamilton's plans because they believed these schemes favored the economic interests of a privileged, urban few at the expense of the majority of Americans, who were farmers. Therefore, for their party label, they combined *Democratic*, to separate themselves from Federalist "elitists," with *Republican*, to accuse Hamilton of plotting a return to monarchical government either by reuniting the United States with the British Empire or by creating a new social and economic aristocracy in the nation in violation of Article I, Section 9, of the Constitution ("No Title of Nobility shall be granted by the United States"). Standing Madison's argument in "Federalist #10" on its head, Jefferson and Madison preached that a minority, monarchical faction had seized control of the nation by controlling President George Washington's prestige and respect, and that Hamilton and Washington hid their own selfish purposes under the thin façade of national unity.

On the eve of the presidential election of 1796, Jefferson gave full rein to his anger and disappointment in a letter to Philip Mazzei, a former Italian émigré who became for a time Jefferson's neighbor in Virginia before returning to Italy in 1785. "It would give you a fever," Jefferson wrote to his friend, to learn about the existence of "an Anglican monarchical aristocratical party . . . whose avowed object is to draw over us the substance, as they have already done the forms, of the British government." In a fully transparent allusion to Washington, Jefferson referred to "apostates who have gone over to these heresies, men who were Samsons in the field and Solomons in the council, but who have had their heads shorn by the harlot England. In short, we are likely to preserve the liberty we have obtained only by unremitting labors and perils. But we shall preserve it. . . . We have only to awake and snap the Lilliputian cords with which they have been entangling us during the first sleep which succeeded our labors."[6]

Unfortunately for Jefferson, Madison, and the other Democratic-Republicans, it took four years and a bitterly contested fight in the House of Representatives in March 1801, in which Jefferson and Aaron Burr tied for electoral votes, before Jefferson wrested control of the presidency from the Federalists. The tone of his first inaugural address may sound conciliatory: "Let us restore to social intercourse that harmony and affection without which liberty and even life itself are but dreary things. . . . We have called by different names brethren of the same principle. We are all republicans—we are all federalists." Privately, however, he viewed his election as a popular mandate to halt Hamilton's design to undermine the Constitution. Writing in September 1819 to Virginian justice Spencer Roane, Jefferson dubbed his election in 1801 "as real a revolution in the principles of our government as that of 1776 was in its form; . . . effected . . . by the rational and peaceable instrument of reform, the suffrage of the people. The nation declared its will by dismissing functionaries of one principle, and electing those of another."[7]

As president, Jefferson served both as chief executive and as head of his now ascendant political party. Jefferson managed his cabinet and Congress much more assertively than had either Washington or John Adams, his two predecessors. He did so through frequent conversations, often inviting Democratic-Republican members to dinner to discuss important legislation. As congressmen and cabinet members dined and enjoyed Jefferson's fine collection of French wines, the president planned strategy with them and used his personal influence to sway them to his side of issues. Put succinctly, party loyalty ruled the actions of the national government, and Jefferson dominated the actions of the party.[8]

Unfortunately for Jefferson, early in his second administration, as warfare between Great Britain and France resumed and entered a far more dangerous phase for Americans, the Federalist Party revived itself. In October 1805, the British victory in the Battle of Trafalgar made the Royal Navy master of the seas, and the French victory at Austerlitz two months later made France ruler of the land. Caught between the British "shark" and the French "tiger," the United States found that options of remaining independent during the wars of Europe receded. Partisanship fed on these foreign policy developments.

Federalist strength increased in New England during the total boycott on foreign trade (see chapter 5) established by Congress in 1807, it continued to grow during Jefferson's last years in office with the Federalist argument that the embargo hurt the region's economy, and it further blossomed during the War of 1812. This revival of the Federalist Party's fortunes frustrated the former president as he worried that its leaders were using foreign policy divisions to regain their partisan influence in the nation. In a January 1813 letter, Jefferson conceded that "each party endeavors to get into the administration of the government, and exclude the other from power . . . and may be stated as a motive of action: but this is only secondary [to] . . . a real and radical difference of political principle. I sincerely wish," he continued, "our differences were but personally who should govern, and that the principles of our constitution were those of both parties. Unfortunately, it is otherwise; and the question of preference between monarchy and republicanism, which has so long divided mankind elsewhere, threatens a permanent division here."[9]

Only with the end of the war and the disappearance of the Federalist Party in its aftermath did Jefferson sense that the nation had turned an important corner by harnessing partisan contentions. Writing to Lafayette in May 1817, Jefferson said that the "best effect" of the war had been "the complete suppression of party. The federalists who were truly American, and their great mass was so, have separated from their brethren who were mere Anglomen [blind supporters of Great Britain], and are received with cordiality into the republican ranks. . . . The evanition of party dissensions has harmonized intercourse, and sweetened society beyond imagination."[10]

His optimism about the disappearance of parties, however, was short-lived. Political divisions in the nation surrounding whether to admit

Missouri, into which slaveholders had taken their slaves, as a state caused him much turmoil. In an April 1820 letter to Massachusetts congressman John Holmes, he likened the Missouri question to "a fire-bell in the night [that] awakened and filled me with terror. I considered it at once the knell of the Union." In December, Jefferson confided to former treasury secretary Albert Gallatin that the introduction of the Missouri bill into Congress was due to the efforts of former Federalists to use the slavery question to revive party divisions in the nation. "The Federalists compleatly put down, and despairing of ever rising again under the old division of whig and tory [republican versus monarchical government], devised a new one, of slave-holding, & non-slave-holding states, which . . . was . . . calculated to give them ascendancy by debauching their old opponents to a coalition with them."[11]

Two years later, Jefferson wrote to US Supreme Court justice William Johnson that the national government—under the rulings of John Marshall's Supreme Court and other Federalist judges that John Adams had appointed during his last days in office—was systematically destroying powers the Constitution had reserved to the states. Sounding very much like a latter-day Antifederalist, Jefferson wrote that the "amalgamation" of the two parties following the Battle of New Orleans at the end of the War of 1812 had been in name only and that "new Republicans" in Congress had begun "preaching the doctrines of the old Federalists." "[F]inding that monarchy is a desperate wish in this country," he wrote, "they rally to the point which they think next best, a consolidated government. Their aim is now therefore to break down the rights reserved by the constitution to the states as a bulwark against that consolidation, the fear of which produced the whole of the opposition to the constitution at it's birth. . . . I scarcely know myself which is most to be deprecated, a consolidation, or dissolution of the states. The horrors of both are beyond the reach of human foresight."[12]

In summary, Jefferson questioned the utility of political parties for the nation during debates over the ratification of the Constitution but then convinced himself in the 1790s that the nation needed the Democratic-Republican Party to save the nation from Hamilton's Federalist agenda and held tightly to these views following his retirement from the presidency. He likened Federalists to the Grecian Hydra, capable of growing two new heads for every one it lost. In his thinking, Federalists had accepted the Constitution only because they had been thwarted from instituting monarchy at the Constitutional Convention. Refusing to accept this situation as final, Hamilton worked as treasury secretary to unravel the work of the convention by creating an all-powerful national government as a stepping-stone to monarchy, led by a partisan faction.

The election of 1800 arrested this attempt, but opposition in the New England states to the embargo of 1807 allowed Federalists to regain power there. The end of the nation's foreign policy problems at the conclusion of the War of 1812 again nearly dealt a deathblow to the Federalists' hopes of regaining power, and following the election of 1816, Jefferson cheered the arrival of the "Era of Good Feelings," so-called because of the end of partisan rivalry for the presidency. Before long, however, he fretted that a cadre of neo-Federalists was using their strength in the slavery question and the judiciary to cement the national government's powers over the states. At the time of his death, he believed that the need for his party was as strong as ever.

II

In retrospect, it is possible to say that Jefferson's fears surrounding the Missouri Compromise blinded him to the fact that political party divisions in the nation had entered a new phase. To increase their unity of purpose, beginning with the presidential election of 1800, Democratic-Republicans in Congress met in caucus to select the party's candidate for president: Jefferson in 1800 and 1804, Madison in 1808 and 1812, and James Monroe in 1816 and 1820. In the presidential election of 1824, however, sectional interests destroyed party unity, and caucus nominee William H. Crawford ran a distant fourth in the popular vote behind Andrew Jackson, John Quincy Adams, and Henry Clay, and he came in third in electoral votes behind Jackson and Adams. Because no candidate received a majority of the electoral votes, the House of Representatives decided the election as it had in 1801, each state casting one vote. Although he had received the largest number of electoral and popular votes, Andrew Jackson saw the House give the presidency to Adams, who immediately appointed Henry Clay as his secretary of state (so many men who held this position had become president that it had become known as the stepping-stone to the White House).

Alleging that a corrupt bargain between Adams and Clay had deprived him of the presidency, Jackson created a new political party to organize a run for the presidency in 1828. To emphasize the fact that there was only one party following the presidential election of 1816, supporters of President

James Monroe had dropped the tag of Democratic from their party name and called it the National Republican Party. Jackson—the hero of the Battle of New Orleans—would never have called himself a Federalist, so he chose the name Democratic (first used in the election of 1832) for his new party to emphasize the fact that the people's will that he be president had been thwarted in 1824.

In creating this new political party, Jackson found support from New Yorker Martin Van Buren, who instilled discipline in the fledgling organization. Van Buren emphasized that Democratic Party members should eschew sectionalist loyalties by choosing the presidential and vice presidential candidates from different regions and by uniting behind the person with the best chance of winning the presidency. He also led the way in New York by supporting efforts to write a new state constitution that greatly expanded the size of the electorate by dropping property qualifications for voting. In Washington, DC, Massachusetts senator Daniel Webster and Kentucky senator Henry Clay, among others, created an opposition party to President Jackson. Rejecting the older but baggage-laden names of Federalist and Republican, supporters of the new party called themselves Whigs to emphasize their position that President Jackson was acting like a king by vetoing congressional legislation, favoring his friends and cronies, and pursuing economic policies that stifled the nation's growth.

Lincoln developed an early attachment to the Whig Party primarily for economic reasons, especially because of its emphasis on internal improvements to facilitate trade that promoted an alliance of New England manufacturing interests and commercial farmers in the South and West (see chapter 6). The Whigs had an early success in the presidential election of 1840 by electing Indian fighter William Henry Harrison, but his successor, slaveholder John Tyler, who strongly supported the South's right to expand into western lands, created rifts in the party. In 1844, Henry Clay became the Whigs' nominee for president in the hopes that Clay, who was a slaveholder but also one of the founders of the American Colonization Society, might reunite the party. Clay narrowly lost the election to Democratic nominee James K. Polk by a vote of 170 to 105 when the state of New York's 36 votes went to Polk. Subtracting those votes from Polk's total and adding them to Clay's would have made the Whig nominee president.[13]

The Whigs managed to avoid the problems that the slavery issue might have presented to the party in 1844 by nominating Mexican War hero

Zachary Taylor as their candidate in the presidential election of 1848. Taylor was a slaveholder who, as the commander of US forces that began the war with Mexico, did not criticize Polk's expansionist policies. Having long served in the US Army, he was also an ardent nationalist. The slavery question instead ended up hurting Democratic candidate Lewis Cass of Michigan, whom many Northerners believed to be proslavery. Anti-Cass supporters bolted the party, forming the Free Soil Party, dedicated to keeping slavery out of the territories, and selecting former Democratic president Martin Van Buren as their candidate. Although Van Buren won no electoral votes, he likely took enough votes from Cass in Northern states to allow Taylor to win by the narrow margin of 163 to 127 electoral votes.

As a member of the House of Representatives from Illinois, Lincoln—as did most Whigs—severely criticized the Polk administration for provoking war with Mexico (see chapter 5) and supported attempts to exclude slavery from the territories taken from Mexico at the war's conclusion. Even though Taylor was a slaveholder, party unity trumped the slavery question for Lincoln, as for most Northern Whigs in the election of 1848. Lincoln confided to one correspondent in February, "I am in favor of Gen: Taylor as the whig candidate for the Presidency because I am satisfied we can elect him, that he would give us a whig administration, and that we can not elect any other whig." He advised another, "[Y]ou should simply go for Genl. Taylor; because by this, you can take some democrats, and lose no whigs; but if you go also for Mr. Polk on the origin and mode of prossecuting the war, you will still take some democrats, but you will lose more whigs, so that in the sum of the opperation you will be loser." To Whigs who wanted to renominate Clay in 1848 instead of Taylor, Lincoln advised them that Clay could not be elected, but Taylor could. "Mr. Clay's chance for an election, is just no chance at all," he wrote in April. "[Clay] might get New-York; and that would have elected [him] in 1844, but it will not now; because he must now, at the least, lose Tennessee, which he had then. . . . In my judgment, we can elect nobody but Gen; Taylor; and we can not elect him without a nomination."[14]

Lincoln was one of those who attended the Whig National Convention that nominated Taylor, and he predicted to his law partner in June that Taylor's nomination promised to attract enough disaffected Democratic voters beyond Whigs to produce "a most overwhelming, glorious, triumph. . . . This is important, if in nothing else, in showing which way the wind blows." In nominating a Mexican War hero, but one who took issues with its commencement, Lincoln believed that Taylor's nomination had "turn[ed] the war thunder against [the Democrats]. The war is now to them, the gallows of Haman, which they built for us, and on which they are doomed to be hanged themselves."[15]

Whig political fortunes suffered a significant blow in July 1850, however, when Taylor died and Vice President Millard Fillmore became president. Fillmore signed a new Fugitive Slave Act that was part of the Compromise of 1850, costing him the support of some Northern Whigs, and he was reluctant to support economic measures that congressional Whigs promoted. Party faithful therefore refused to give the incumbent president the party's nomination for the presidential election of 1852 and instead nominated Winfield Scott as its candidate, hoping to repeat the successful strategy that had produced Taylor's success in 1848. Although Democratic candidate Franklin Pierce won a bare majority of the popular vote, Scott carried just four states with 42 electoral votes against 252 for Pierce. Lincoln's papers reveal only lukewarm interest in the election compared with prior or subsequent ones; he spoke twice to the Springfield Scott Club in August 1852 and once in Peoria.[16]

Henry Clay's death in June 1852 provided Lincoln with the opportunity to encapsulate the change in the nation that had occurred between Jefferson's time and his own regarding the role of political parties in the nation. "A free people," he said, "in times of peace and quiet—when pressed by no common danger—naturally divide into parties. At such times, the man who is of neither party, is not—cannot be, of any consequence. Mr. Clay, therefore, was of a party." Continuing the theme that political parties were an inevitable outgrowth of human nature, Lincoln emphasized in his eulogy that political parties were instruments formed by like-minded people to advance issues that they believed benefited the nation. Clay, Lincoln explained, attached himself to a political party because "he burned with a zeal for [his nation's] advancement, prosperity and glory. . . . He desired the prosperity of his countrymen . . . chiefly to show to the world that freemen could be prosperous."[17]

Illinois senator Stephen A. Douglas's introduction of the Kansas-Nebraska Act in January 1854 led to a realignment of party allegiances. Southern Whigs increasingly abandoned the party, and opposition to the expansion of slavery into national territories heretofore declared off-limits to slavery by the Missouri Compromise further increased the appeal of third parties in the North that sought to keep slavery out of these areas. One such group took as its name the second portion of Jefferson's Democratic-Republican Party, which had ceased to exist in the 1830s with the creation of Jackson's Democratic Party and the Whigs. Illinois proponents of the newly formed Republican Party tabbed Lincoln in November 1854 as a possible leader of their cause by inviting him to attend a meeting of the state's Republican Central Committee in Chicago. Lincoln responded to an organizer of the meeting, "I have been perplexed some to understand why my name was placed on that committee. I was not consulted on the subject; nor was I apprized of the appointment, until I discovered it by accident two or three weeks afterwards."[18]

At least part of Lincoln's reluctance to become associated with the new organization was based on the fact that it was still in the process of defining its views on the issues of the day, especially slavery. "I suppose my opposition to the principle of slavery is as strong as that of any member of the Republican party," Lincoln continued, "but I had also supposed that the *extent* to which I feel authorized to carry that opposition, practically [opposing only the expansion of slavery in the territories and not the existence of the institution where it already operated]; was not at all satisfactory to that party."[19] Writing the following August to Owen Lovejoy, brother of the abolitionist Elijah Lovejoy, who had been killed by a proslavery mob in 1837, Lincoln shared, "Not even *you* are more anxious to prevent the extension of slavery than I; and yet the political atmosphere is such, just now, that I fear to do any thing, lest I do wrong." Specifically, Lincoln worried that the Republican Party would not grow its members until third parties in the Northern states disappeared. "We can not get them [new members] so long as they cling to a hope of success under their own organization; and I fear an open push by us now, may offend them, and tend to prevent our ever getting them. About us here, they are mostly my old political and personal friends; and I have hoped their organization would die out without the painful necessity of my taking an open stand against them." [20] In a contemporary letter to his old friend Joshua F. Speed, now living in Kentucky, Lincoln wrote, "You enquire where I now stand. That is a disputed point. I think I am a whig; but others say there are no whigs, and that I am an abolitionist . . . [because] I now do no more than oppose the *extension* of slavery."[21]

By the summer of 1856, however, Lincoln was steadfastly within the Republican Party camp and campaigning for the election of John C. Frémont as president. In dramatic contrast to his laissez-faire attitude during the election of 1852, Lincoln traversed the state of Illinois and spoke also in Michigan in favor of the Republican Party candidate.[22] As a further measure of the distance that he had traveled from his Whig Party affiliation, in these speeches Lincoln urged old Whigs to drop support for Millard Fillmore and unite with the Republicans behind Frémont. Following the election, he blamed Whig divisions between Fillmore and Frémont for Frémont's defeat. "All of us who did not vote for Mr. [James] Buchanan," he said, "taken together, are a majority of four hundred thousand. . . . Can we not come together, for the future[?] . . . Thus let bygones be bygones. Let past differences, as nothing be."[23] Writing to "a Fillmore man" in August, Lincoln cautioned him that a vote for Fillmore in Illinois was the equivalent of a vote for Buchanan. "Does any one pretend that Fillmore can carry the vote of this State? I have not heared a single man pretend so. . . . The Buchanan men see this; and hence their great anxiety in favor of the Fillmore movement."[24]

Lincoln's calculations were accurate. Buchanan received 174 votes to Frémont's 114, while Fillmore received only 8. All of Frémont's electoral votes came from Northern states, and if he had carried Buchanan's home state of Pennsylvania and either Illinois or Indiana, Frémont would have become president. In a fragment relating to the formation of the Republican Party that Lincoln wrote in early 1857, he reflected on the election and the circumstances leading to the formation of the Republican Party: "The Republican . . . party is newly formed; and in forming, old party ties had to be broken, and the attractions of party pride, and influential leaders were wholly wanting. In spite of old differences, prejudices, and animosities, it's members . . . formed and manouvered in the face of the deciplined enemy, and in the teeth of all his persistent misrepresentations. . . . That army is, to-day, the best hope of the nation, and of the world. Their work is before them; and from which they may not guiltlessly turn away."[25]

Lincoln did not "turn away." Rather, in celebrated debates against Stephen A. Douglas in 1858 across Illinois, at Cooper Institute in New York City in February 1860, and in subsequent speeches in New England, Lincoln confidently raised the Republican Party's standard. At the time of his Cooper Institute address, Lincoln was optimistic that the party had coalesced behind the issues that would be successful in the presidential election of 1860. In

Figure 2.1. Campaign button for Abraham Lincoln and Hannibal Hamlin, 1860 presidential election. *Mathew B. Brady, photographer. Library of Congress.*

his speech, reported in Republican newspapers across the Northern states, he asked the party faithful not to be swayed in their determination by false arguments from Southerners that the Republicans had created a sectional party, that the party was run by abolitionists, or that the Republicans were intent on destroying the nation. "You [Southerners] say we are sectional. . . . You produce your proof; and what is it? Why, that our party has no existence in your section—gets no votes in your section. . . . The fact that we get no votes in your section, is a fact of your making, and not of ours."[26]

He continued this theme during the time leading up to his election to the presidency and following it. Writing in November 1860 to a Connecticut Republican, Lincoln refused to repeat himself on the issues of the day under the belief that everyone who wanted to know his positions on these points could. "To press a repetition" of his views, he wrote, "upon those who *have* listened, is useless; to press it upon those who have *refused* to listen, and still refuse, would be wanting in self-respect, and would have an appearance of sycophancy and timidity, which would excite the contempt of good men, and encourage bad ones to clamor the more loudly."[27] In a speech at the Astor House in New York City in February 1861, on his way to his inauguration,

Lincoln further clarified why he had remained silent about his views during and subsequent to the election: "I have kept silence for the reason that I supposed it was peculiarly proper that I should do so until the time came when, according to the customs of the country, I should speak officially."[28] That time came on March 4, 1861, when he delivered his first inaugural address. Nowhere in the speech did he mention either the Democratic or Republican Party, but he laid the issue of civil war directly on those who were "dissatisfied" with the current state of affairs. "In *your* hands, . . . and not in *mine*, is the momentous issue of civil war. The government will not assail *you*. You can have no conflict, without being yourselves the aggressors."[29]

Without specifically saying so, the inaugural address brought Lincoln closer to Jefferson's understanding of political parties than to the devotion to pluralism that Lincoln had touted in his eulogy to Clay. By implication, Southerners and Southern sympathizers were members of factions in the meaning attached to that word by Jefferson because they were dividing the nation rather than working to keep it together. In his Cooper Institute speech, Lincoln referred to Republicans as "conservatives" because they were trying to save the nation and Southerners as "radicals" because they were intent on destroying it.[30] Without repeating the wording in his first inaugural, Lincoln's message was the same.

Ignoring the fact that he was a minority president because he had won only 40 percent of the popular vote in the election of 1860, receiving 1,865,908 votes compared with 2,819,653 for the other candidates, Lincoln strengthened his attachment to his party during the war as the only one seeking national unity, thereby moving him even closer to Jefferson's belief that Federalists practiced divisive politics solely for partisan advantage. In a proclamation revoking the May 1862 Order of Military Emancipation for slaves in Georgia, Florida, and South Carolina by General David Hunter, who was a strong advocate for arming African Americans in the war, Lincoln appealed "earnestly" to the slaveholders of those states that they not "be blind to the signs of the times. I beg of you a calm and enlarged consideration of them, ranging, if it may be, far above personal and partizan politics."[31]

Similarly, in responding to criticisms of his suspension of the writ of habeas corpus (see also chapter 5), Lincoln wrote letters in June 1863 not only defending his action but also directly addressing the issue of partisanship in the Democratic Party. To Erastus Corning and others in Albany, New York, Lincoln wrote:

I can not overlook the fact that the meeting speak[s] as "Democrats" . . . rather than "American citizens." In this time of national peril I would have preferred to meet you upon a level one step higher than any party platform; because I am sure that from such more elevated position, we could do better battle for the country we all love, than we possibly can from those lower ones, where from the force of habit, the prejudices of the past, and selfish hopes of the future, we are sure to expend much of our ingenuity and strength, in finding fault with, and aiming blows at each other.[32]

Lincoln's disappointment with those who would not support his policies to reunite the nation was not limited to Democrats but also extended to members of his own party who opposed the administration's policies. For example, Republican Party losses in the midterm elections of 1862 caused some party faithful to lay the blame at the feet of the president in his failure to suppress the rebellion. Lincoln wrote to one of these that he was sensitive to the fact "that if the war fails, the administration fails, and that I *will* be blamed for it, whether I deserve it or not. And I ought to be blamed, if I could do better. You think I could do better; therefore you blame me already. I think I could not do better; therefore I blame you for blaming me." In the field of battle, Lincoln continued, he saw no difference in actions between those who supported the administration and those who opposed it. "In sealing their faith with their blood . . . republicans, did all that men could do; but did they any more than . . . some . . . [who] have been bitterly, and repeatedly, denounced to me as secession sympathizers?"[33]

Other Republicans, including some of Lincoln's friends in Illinois, opposed his issuance of the Emancipation Proclamation. Writing to one of these in August 1863, Lincoln offered this judgment: "You say you will not fight to free negroes. Some of them seem willing to fight for you; but no manner. Fight you, then, exclusively to save the Union [because] I issued the proclamation on purpose to aid you in saving the Union."[34] The open rift with members of his party escalated in December 1863 when Lincoln issued his Proclamation of Amnesty and Reconstruction and addressed the topic of Reconstruction in his annual message to Congress. "[W]hy," he asked rhetorically, "any proclamation now upon this subject? This question is beset with the conflicting views that the step might be delayed too long or be taken too soon. In some States the elements for [rejoining the Union] seem ready for action, but remain inactive, apparently for want of a rallying point—a plan of action. . . . By the proclamation a plan is presented which may be accepted by them as a rallying point, and which they are assured in advance will not be rejected here."[35]

Some members of his own party disliked Lincoln's plan allowing Southerners to reorganize their state governments when 10 percent of the voters in 1860 had sworn an oath of allegiance to the United States because they believed that Southerners should be punished for causing the war. On July 2, 1864, Congress passed what came to be known as the Wade-Davis Bill, asserting its control over the issue of Reconstruction and requiring stricter proof of adherence to the Union, with an oath of past and future allegiance as opposed to Lincoln's proposal of an oath of only future allegiance. Lincoln would not sign the bill, he wrote, because he refused to annul state constitutions and governments already installed in Arkansas and Louisiana under his plan, "thereby repelling and discouraging the loyal citizens who have set up the same, as to further effort."[36]

In days leading up to the presidential election of 1864, Lincoln continued to emphasize that his administration was devoted to resurrecting the Union. In September, he wrote to General William Tecumseh Sherman suggesting that the general give soldiers leave in order to go home to vote in the upcoming state elections. In his letter to Sherman, Lincoln highlighted the importance of the state of Indiana to the war effort with these words: "[T]he loss of it to the friends of the Government would go far towards losing the whole Union cause. The bad effect upon the November election, and especially the giving the State Government to those who will oppose the war in every possible way, are too much to risk, if it can possibly be avoided." Because Indiana was "the only important State, voting in October, whose soldiers cannot vote in the field," he asked Sherman to do anything he could "safely do to let her soldiers, or any part of them, go home and vote at the State election."[37] Addressing the 189th New York Volunteers on October 24, 1864, on their way to the front, Lincoln said, "While others differ with the Administration, and, perhaps, honestly, the soldiers generally have sustained it; they have not only fought right, but, so far as could be judged from their actions, they have voted right, and I for one thank you for it."[38]

Following the election, Lincoln downplayed his personal victory in order to emphasize the fact that—in his mind—the nation would endure. On

November 8, the president said that he valued the support of everyone who had voted "on behalf of the Union organization, [because they] have wrought for the best interests of their country and the world, not only for the present, but for all future ages. . . . I give thanks to the Almighty for this evidence of the people's resolution to stand by free government and the rights of humanity."[39]

In his last public speech—three days before his assassination—Lincoln gave thanks for the end of the war but noted that it was embarrassing "that we, the loyal people, differ among ourselves as to the mode, manner, and means of reconstruction. . . . Let us all join in doing the acts necessary to restoring the proper practical relations between these states and the Union." He acknowledged that various plans for Reconstruction might accomplish the goal of reuniting the nation, but he closed with the hope that each state might find a unique solution to the problem. "What has been said of Louisiana will apply generally to other States. And yet so great peculiarities pertain to each state; and such important and sudden changes occur in the same state; and, withal, so new and unprecedented is the whole case, that no exclusive, and inflexible plan can safely be prescribed as to details and colatterals." In words that cannot be definitively interpreted because of his too sudden demise, Lincoln opened the door to a reconfiguration of political parties if members of his own party persisted in their opposition to a reconciliation on the terms he had proposed in December 1863. "In the present 'situation' as the phrase goes," he said, "it may be my duty to make some new announcement to the people of the South. I am considering, and shall not fail to act, when satisfied that action will be proper."[40]

III

In summary, a cynic might say that partisans will always view themselves as working for the nation's welfare and label their opponents as factions intent on subverting the general will. Although Jefferson convinced himself that Federalists were monarchists in order to justify a need for an opposition political party, in fact Federalists and Democratic-Republicans divided over policy issues—especially the powers of the national government relative to the states (chapter 3) or whether commerce and industry were preferable to agriculture as the economic basis of the nation (chapter 6). Jefferson also accused neo-Federalists of using the Missouri Compromise to promote sectional discord for the purpose of partisan political gain, a charge that Lincoln later leveled against Democrats and members of his own party during the Civil War. Late in his life, however, Lincoln's attachment to partisan solidarity cooled as he faced the prospect of reuniting the nation in the war's aftermath, and based on Radical Republicans' opposition to his plans for Reconstruction, he questioned whether his political party was capable of accomplishing that task.

Several other partisan realignments have taken place since 1865—most notably in 1896, 1932, and perhaps 1980—and the two-party system continues to operate in the nation. Still, Americans often question whether political parties are necessary entities or merely evils for organizing political differences. In this way, the experiences of Jefferson and Lincoln with political parties provide context for current discussions without settling the issue.

------------{ Chapter Three }------------

"WHENCE THIS MAGICAL OMNIPOTENCE
OF 'STATE RIGHTS' . . . ?"

In Michael Shaara's Pulitzer Prize–winning novel about the Battle of Gettysburg, *The Killer Angels*, Mainer Joshua Lawrence Chamberlain talks
with his brother Tom about a conversation that Tom had with three Rebel
prisoners: "We asked them why they were fighting this war, thinkin' on
slavery and all, and one fella said they was fightin' for their 'rats.' Hee. That's
what he said. . . . It finally dawned on me that what the feller meant was
their 'rights,' only, the way they talk, it came out 'rats.' Hee. Then after that
I asked this fella what rights he had that we were offendin', and he said, well,
he didn't know, but he must have some rights he didn't know nothin' about."[1]

Debate over the extent and nature of states' rights has ebbed and flowed
throughout the nation's history and is especially shrill today. Both Thomas
Jefferson and Abraham Lincoln subscribed to the belief that the Constitution
created a federal system of government, in which the powers of government
are shared between the national government and the states, and thereby gave
rights to states, but they approached the meaning of federalism from opposite perspectives. Jefferson believed that the Tenth Amendment prevented
the national government from exercising sole authority to decide the param-
eters of its powers. Abraham Lincoln, by way of contrast, denied that states
had the last word in settling disputes between themselves and the nation.

Both men also addressed the issue of whether a state or states had the
right to secede from the nation if they felt that their "rats" were being
withheld or denied. Taken together, Jefferson's and Lincoln's thinking on
these issues—especially points where there appear to be agreements and
disagreements—provide important perspectives from which to gauge current controversies over states' rights, nullification, and secession.

I

Under the nation's first form of government, the Articles of Confederation (1781–89), each of the thirteen states exercised "sovereignty, freedom, and independence, and every Power, Jurisdiction, and right, which [was] not by this confederation expressly delegated to the United States, in Congress assembled." Although the states bound themselves under the articles "in perpetual Union," in practice each state defined and acted on what best served its interests. The US Constitution (1789–) changed the demarcation between state and national authority by harking back to the Declaration of Independence and its assertion that the people can alter or abolish government. In erecting a higher sovereignty than states—the people of the United States—the framers of the Constitution paved the way for expanding the powers of the national government significantly, thereby diminishing the influence of states.[2] Then, in ratifying the Tenth Amendment—"The powers not delegated to the United States by the Constitution, nor prohibited by it to the States, are reserved to the States respectively, or to the people"—in 1791, states attempted to safeguard their powers in areas not specifically assigned to the national government.

Thomas Jefferson did not participate in discussions leading to the drafting of the Articles of Confederation because he served as a member of the Virginia Assembly from 1776 until 1779, when he became governor of the state (1779–81). As an assemblyman, he focused his attention on local concerns, especially revising Virginia's laws to purge them of British influences. As governor, he steadfastly asserted state sovereignty against national attempts to force the states to more directly support the nation's war efforts.

Although it comes as a great surprise to many Americans, Jefferson had no hand in writing the Constitution either, as he was serving as minister to France during the Constitutional Convention.[3] Delegates to the convention bound themselves to strict silence during their deliberations, so the first Jefferson heard of the details of the document came to him courtesy of John Adams and Adams's son-in-law William Stephens Smith in London, as well as his Virginian neighbor James Madison—commonly referred to as the "Father of the Constitution" because of his leading role in the debates and because he kept a record of the convention's deliberations.

In November 1787, Jefferson fretted to Adams that the proposed House of Representatives "will not be adequate to the management of affairs either foreign or federal," and he disapproved of the fact that presidents (prior to ratification of the Twenty-Second Amendment in 1951) might be repeatedly reelected every four years and thus become "an officer for life." Jefferson feared that such a possibility would lead foreign nations to meddle in national affairs, and he therefore preferred that presidents serve only one term without the possibility of reelection. Prior to Franklin Delano Roosevelt, presidents—including Jefferson—acceded to his views as first implemented by President George Washington in 1796 by limiting their service to eight years. Jefferson ruminated at the end of his letter to Adams that "all the good of this new constitution might have been couched in three or four new articles to be added to the good, old, and venerable fabrick, which should have been preserved even as a religious relique."[4]

Jefferson repeated his criticism of the reelection of the president in a letter to Madison in December and added that the document needed a bill of rights, "providing clearly & without the aid of sophisms for freedom of religion, freedom of the press," and other protections for the people against government abuse. Indeed, in Jefferson's view, the need of such protection was all the more important in light of the expanded powers of the national government and his recognition that provisions in state constitutions could be overridden by national authority. "[A] bill of rights is what the people are entitled to against every government on earth," he badgered his friend, "general or particular, & what no just government should refuse, or rest on inferences."[5] In subsequent letters, he toyed with the idea of having nine states ratify the Constitution, with the remaining four withholding ratification until a bill of rights was added, but he eventually dropped this plan in favor of having the first Congress take up the matter, as it did.[6]

His reservations about the document notwithstanding, Jefferson accepted George Washington's invitation to join his administration as secretary of state, no doubt bolstered by the fact that Madison had been elected to serve in the House of Representatives. As he undertook his new responsibilities, Jefferson's fears about the dangers of an all-powerful central government escalated as a result of disagreements with Alexander Hamilton's domestic and foreign policy agendas.

One of the primary areas of disagreement between the two men centered on the powers that the national government exercised under Article I, Section 8, of the Constitution. To accomplish his goal of funding the national debt of the United States, Hamilton argued that a national bank was "necessary and proper" in order to carry out its enumerated powers, such as to borrow money, collect taxes, and pay the nation's debts. Jefferson disagreed based on his belief that Article I, Section 8, limited the powers of the national government to specified powers (see chapter 5).

Congress approved of Hamilton's plans, but Jefferson put sufficient doubts in Washington's mind regarding the bank's constitutionality that the president hesitated to sign the bill creating a national bank. Jefferson urged President Washington to veto the legislation. Using the veto power in this instance was appropriate, Jefferson argued, because it was "the shield provided by the constitution to protect against the invasions of the legislature." In Jefferson's mind, the presidential veto had been specifically created "for cases where [members of Congress] are clearly misled by error, ambition, or interest."[7]

Washington's failure to take Jefferson's advice and veto the legislation marked a turning point in Jefferson's relationship with the president. In a February 1792 letter to Washington, Jefferson accused Hamilton of using the national bank bill and his plan for funding the debt of the United States as a way of "creating an influence of his department over the members of the legislature. . . . These were no longer the votes then of the representatives of the people, but of deserters from the rights & interests of the people: & it was impossible to consider their decisions, which had nothing in view but to enrich themselves, as the measures of the fair majority, which ought always to be respected." In addition to accusing Hamilton of bribing members of Congress to support his financial plans, Jefferson wrote to Washington that Hamilton "wishes the general government should have power to make laws binding the states in all cases whatsoever," thereby setting aside the Tenth Amendment.[8]

Contemporaneously with this letter, Jefferson began to keep notes of conversations he had with Washington and others in bound notebooks, published after his death as the "Anas." In these recapitulations, Jefferson wrote that Washington had discussed with him the possibility of retiring from the presidency in 1792. In addition to having a desire to leave public service, Washington told Jefferson that he "was sensible too of a decay of his hearing [and] perhaps his other faculties might fall off & he not be sensible of it."[9] Reflecting on these conversations in 1818, Jefferson intimated in his "Anas" that Hamilton was taking advantage of Washington's loss of faculties and senility: "[Washington's] memory was already sensibly impaired by age, the firm tone of mind for which he had been remarkable, was beginning to relax, it's energy was abated; a listlessness of labor, a desire for tranquillity had crept on him, and a willingness to let others act and even think for him."[10] Convinced that Hamilton was using Washington to undermine the constitutional limits imposed on the national government and direct the actions of the nation for the benefit of himself and his friends, Jefferson left his post as secretary of state at the end of 1793 and went home to Monticello.

He was not out of office for long. In the presidential election of 1796, John Adams received three more electoral votes than Jefferson and was elected president. Before the Twelfth Amendment altered the method for choosing the president and vice president, Jefferson—as the second-highest vote getter—became vice president. Although Adams and Jefferson had developed a friendship during their service in the Second Continental Congress that carried over to their time as ministers to England and France, respectively, in the 1780s, the events of Washington's administration drove a wedge between the two men. They did begin corresponding with one another following the War of 1812, but when Jefferson composed his 1818 "explanation" of the materials in the "Anas," he characterized Adams as "originally . . . a republican," but said that the "glare of royalty and nobility, during his mission to England, had made him believe their fascination a necessary ingredient in government."[11]

Chief among Jefferson's criticisms of the Adams presidency was Congress's passage of—and Adams's failure to veto—acts that allowed the president to deport noncitizens and that attempted to muzzle newspaper criticisms of the administration, known as the Alien and Sedition Acts. Integral to Jefferson's opposition to these acts was his belief that—under the First and Tenth Amendments—the laws passed by Congress were unconstitutional. He also questioned the right of the national government to convene grand juries to bring indictments against individuals accused of breaking the laws, believing that these tribunals could be convened only by local authorities in the states where the alleged violations occurred.[12] His anger concerning these actions overflowed into his Kentucky Resolutions, which he drafted in October 1798.

In arguing that Congress had overstepped its constitutional boundaries when it passed the two acts, Jefferson wrote that "the several States composing the United States of America . . . constituted a General Government for special purposes [and] delegated to that government certain definite powers, reserving, each State to itself, the residuary mass of right to their own self-government." Therefore, whenever "the General Government assumes undelegated powers, its acts are unauthoritative, void, and of no force." In times "of greater tranquillity," Jefferson urged, the Constitution should be amended to specify how the proceedings of the national government might be judged to be outside of the powers granted under the Constitution, but in this circumstance, "every State has a natural right . . . to nullify of their own authority all assumptions of power by others within their limits: that without this right, they would be under the dominion, absolute and unlimited, of whosoever might exercise this right of judgment for them."[13] Thirty years later, South Carolinian John C. Calhoun used this language to justify his Doctrine of Nullification and, eventually, the right of a state to secede from the Union.

For several reasons, a close reading of Jefferson's Kentucky Resolutions promotes doubts that they were the forerunners to Calhoun's doctrines. First, Jefferson was correct when he wrote that no mechanism existed under the Constitution for judging in cases of disputed authority when either the national government or the states exceeded their powers. To do so, in his view, would have made these decisions discretionary on the part of these entities, thereby undercutting the Constitution's role as the supreme law of the land. In 1803, Chief Justice John Marshall asserted that the Supreme Court had the power to review congressional legislation to see whether it conformed to the Constitution, but Jefferson never accepted the authority of that judgment and defied at least part of a subsequent Marshall ruling during the Burr Trial in 1807 that the court might compel a president to deliver up evidence (see chapter 5). In Jefferson's mind, therefore, this issue was far from settled in 1798 and throughout his lifetime.

Second, Jefferson's theory that the states created the national government and used the Constitution to limit the national government to "certain definite powers" reads the Constitution backward from the position of the Tenth Amendment rather than forward from the Constitutional Convention. Integral to this view is the wording of the Kentucky Resolutions where Jefferson said that in limiting the powers of the national government, "each State acceded as a State, and is an integral party, its co-States forming, as to itself, the other party."[14] Viewed in this way, the federal division of powers accomplished under the Constitution did not differentiate between a national government and states acting alone, but rather a national government and the states acting together. A grammatical point is useful in this context: the issue was not one of rights residing in individual states (state rights), but rather of rights that belonged to all the states collectively (states' rights). Hence, in a portion of the Kentucky Resolutions that is commonly overlooked, the document envisioned having the Kentucky legislature "communicate the preceding resolutions to the legislatures of the several States; to assure them that this commonwealth continues in the same esteem of their friendship and union which it has manifested from that moment at which a common danger first suggested a common union."[15]

Jefferson's statement, therefore, that "where powers are assumed which have not been delegated, a nullification of the act is the rightful remedy" must be read within the context of the states acting together. When a state believed that the national government had acted in an unconstitutional manner, it would "nullify" a law, but it would be up to the "co-states" to determine whether to "declar[e] these acts void, and of no force." Only then would each state "take measures of its own for providing that neither these acts, nor any others of the General Government not plainly and intentionally authorized by the Constitution, shall be exercised within their respective territories." Once representatives of the "co-states" had corresponded or conferred with one another, that group would "lay their proceedings before the next session of [the Kentucky] Assembly."[16]

Several additional writings of Jefferson—one contemporaneous with the Kentucky Resolutions and three later in his life—corroborate the conclusion that Jefferson's and Calhoun's views on "nullification" were not synonymous, especially as Calhoun used the concept to support the right of a state to secede from the Union. In June 1798, Jefferson wrote to Virginian John Taylor concerning rumors that Virginia and North Carolina might separate from the Union. "It is true," Jefferson conceded, "that we are completely under the saddle of Massachusets & Connecticut, and that they ride us very hard, cruelly insulting our feelings as well as exhausting our strength and substance. . . . But if on a temporary superiority of the one party, the other is to resort to a scission of the Union, no federal government can ever exist." The logical end to secession, in other words, was anarchy, with each state out for itself. "A little patience," Jefferson counseled, "and we shall see the reign of witches pass over, their spells dissolve, and the people, recovering their true sight, restore their government to it's true principles."[17]

Following his presidency, he returned to these ideas in a January 1811 letter to the Frenchman A. L. C. Destutt de Tracy, author of *A Commentary and Review of Montesquieu's Spirit of Laws.* Referring to state governments as "the true barriers of our liberty in this country," Jefferson wrote that the American Revolution and the Constitution "amalgamated [the states] into one as to their foreign concerns, but single and independent as to their internal administration." Despite this happy arrangement, one potential problem still existed—namely, "that certain States from local and occasional discontents, might attempt to secede from the Union. . . . But it is not probable that local discontents can spread to such an extent, . . . and if ever they should reach the majority, they would then become the regular government, acquire the ascendency in Congress, and be able to redress their own grievances by laws peaceably and constitutionally passed."[18]

Two years later, he wrote a similar letter in the wake of fears that the Hartford Convention would propose that the New England states secede from the nation. "At the head of this MINORITY [intent on separation]," he reflected, "is what is called the Essex Junto of Massachusetts. But the MAJORITY of these *leaders* do not aim at separation. In this, they adhere to the known principle of General Hamilton, never, under any views, to break the Union. . . . The moment that these leaders should avowedly propose a separation of the Union, or the establishment of regal government, their popular adherents would quit them to a man, and join the republican standard; and the partisans of this change, even in Massachusetts, would thus find themselves an army of officers without a soldier."[19]

Finally, in a late 1825 letter, Jefferson lamented the actions of the national government under President John Quincy Adams to consolidate all powers unto itself. "Take together the decisions of the federal court, the doctrines of the President, and the misconstructions of the constitutional compact acted on by the legislature of the federal branch, and it is all too evident, that the three ruling branches of that department are in combination to strip their colleagues, the State authorities, of the powers reserved by them, and to exercise themselves all functions foreign and domestic." Nonetheless, he advised against having the states secede from the Union. "That must be the last resource, not to be thought of until much longer and greater sufferings. If every infraction of a compact of so many parties is to be resisted at once, as a dissolution of it, none can ever be formed which would last one year. We must have patience and longer endurance then with our brethren . . . and separate from our companions only when the sole alternatives left, are the dissolution of our Union with them, or submission to a government without limitation of powers."[20]

Perhaps Jefferson's best expression of his views regarding the perpetual union of the states occurs in his autobiography, which he began in 1821. With reference to the Articles of Confederation, he concluded, "Our first essay in America to establish a federative government had fallen, on trial, very short of it's object" because the "instrument" did not bind the states and the people tightly together. "The fundamental defect of the Confederation was that Congress was not authorized to act immediately on the people, & by it's own officers." Because a state legislature could negate of itself "every measure proposed by Congress" for dealing with common issues, the national government became powerless to act. "Yet this state of things afforded a happy augury of the future march of our confederacy," he deduced, "when it was seen that the good sense and good dispositions of the people, as soon as they perceived the incompetence of their first compact, instead of leaving it's correction to insurrection and civil war, agreed with one voice to elect deputies to a general convention, who should peaceably meet and agree on such a constitution as 'would ensure peace, justice, liberty, the common defence & general welfare.'"[21]

This interpretation—that the people of the United States met to write a Constitution that would fashion a federal division of powers between the states and the national government—formed the basis for much of Jefferson's first inaugural address (1801). Believing, as he did, that under Hamilton's leadership the Federalist Party was planning to reinstitute monarchical rule in the nation, Jefferson said that the primary purpose of his administration would be to return the nation to "federal and republican principles, our attachment to union and representative government."[22] In other words, the people had created two governments under the Constitution—that of the states and that of the nation—and had divided the two governments' responsibilities into domestic concerns and national security. Federalism bound the states and the national government into a perpetual union by separating the powers that each group exercised and thereby made secession unnecessary.

II

The issue of the powers of the national government over the states was crucial to Abraham Lincoln's presidential campaign, specifically whether the national government had the power under the Constitution to prohibit the expansion of slavery into federal territories. Lincoln's answer was consistently and unequivocally yes.

In his first major speech on the Kansas-Nebraska Act, at Peoria, Illinois, in October 1854, Lincoln recounted how the Confederation Congress in 1787 in one of its last actions—and the US Congress in one of its first—had created the Northwest Territory and prohibited slavery in it. In succeeding years, Congress had prohibited slaves from being exported to other nations or imported from them, and in 1820, it had prohibited slavery in the Louisiana Purchase territories north of the southern boundary of Missouri. The Kansas-Nebraska Act was, in Lincoln's mind, regressive because it gave new life to the institution, once confined to regions where it already existed, by allowing it in areas where it had been originally excluded (see chapter 1).[23]

The Dred Scott decision (1857) was even more regressive, he told delegates to the Illinois Republican state convention meeting at Springfield in June 1858 in his "House Divided" speech. When the justices affirmed that slavery was a property right under the Fifth Amendment (African Americans, the court ruled, were property, not people), they concluded that Congress had violated this right by passing the Missouri Compromise, which limited the areas into which slaveholders could take their property. "Either," Lincoln said, "the *opponents* of slavery, will arrest the further spread of it, and place it where the public mind shall rest in the belief that it is in course of ultimate extinction; or its *advocates* will push it forward, till it shall become alike lawful in *all* the States, *old* as well as *new*—*North* as well as *South*."[24]

It is not surprising that Southerners understood the "House Divided" speech to be an announcement that Lincoln—or any Republican, if elected president—planned to abolish slavery in the nation. Lincoln was no abolitionist, however, and as a candidate for the presidency, he developed the position of stopping the expansion of slavery while guaranteeing its existence where it already operated as a compromise between the two sides. In fact, he portrayed the Supreme Court as promoting a nationalizing attitude toward slavery by asserting that as a property right under the Fifth Amendment, it was questionable whether *a state* could prohibit its operation.[25] Federalism—the division of authority between the states and the national government that Jefferson so consistently espoused—became Lincoln's answer for how to handle the slavery issue.

In a speech at Columbus, Ohio, in September 1859, Lincoln affirmed his belief "that the States must, without the interference of the general government, do all those things that pertain *exclusively* to themselves—that are local in their nature, that have no connection with the general government."[26] This interpretation of "state rights" would also have been attractive to many Republicans in Wisconsin and other Northern states who used that proposition to support their assertion that the Fugitive Slave Law, which Congress passed to implement provisions of the Compromise of 1850, conflicted with a state's right to protect individual liberty.[27]

Lincoln shone the most dramatic and systematic spotlight on this topic in February 1860 in a speech at the Cooper Institute in New York City. He began his address by trying to convince his audience that throughout their lives a majority of the men who had framed the US Constitution "certainly understood that no proper division of local from federal authority, nor any part of the Constitution, forbade the Federal Government to control slavery in the federal territories." But, Lincoln insisted, the question of the expansion of slavery had to be separated from the reality that the institution already existed in a number of states. Because it existed in certain areas, its existence was a fact that entitled it to remain there, so long as the voting populace of the state wanted it. *"As those fathers marked it, so let it be again marked . . . to be tolerated and protected only because of and so far as its actual presence among us makes that toleration and protection a necessity. Let all the guaranties those fathers gave it, be, not grudgingly, but fully and fairly maintained. For this Republicans contend, and with this, so far as I know or believe, they will be content."*[28]

Addressing Southerners, with the qualification "if they would listen—as I suppose they will not," Lincoln said, "Republican doctrines and declarations are accompanied with a continual protest against any interference whatever with your slaves, or with you about your slaves." He then cited Jefferson and stated that he agreed with him that the national government had no power to emancipate slaves. The crux of the issue lay in disagreements over whether the Constitution allowed slaveholders to take their slaves into federal territories or whether Congress could prohibit such movement. "[N]o such right is specifically written in the Constitution. That instrument is literally silent about any such right. We . . . deny that such a right has any existence in the Constitution, even by implication."[29] But the Supreme Court had ruled otherwise. Lincoln told his New York City audience that the court had acted in error when it ruled that "the right of property in a slave is distinctly and expressly affirmed in the Constitution." Instead,

Lincoln said, "[a]n inspection of the Constitution will show that the right of property in a slave is not '*distinctly* and *expressly* affirmed' in it," because the words *slave, slavery,* and *property* in connection with these words do not appear in the document. "When this obvious mistake of the Judges shall be brought to their notice," he asked rhetorically, "is it not reasonable to expect that they will withdraw the mistaken statement, and reconsider the conclusion based upon it?"[30]

Finally, Lincoln turned to Republicans in the audience and said that it was "*exceedingly desirable*" that all people in the nation should live in harmony with one another. "The question recurs, what will satisfy [Southerners]? Simply this: We must not only let them alone, but we must, somehow, convince them that we do leave them alone. . . . Wrong as we think slavery is, we can yet afford to let it alone where it is, because that much is due to the necessity arising from its actual presence in the nation."[31]

As the Republican candidate for president, Lincoln consistently repeated his message that relied on the logic of federalism, that the powers of the national government—under the Constitution, through legislation passed by Congress—extended to the nation's territories, while at the same time affirming a state's right to decide domestic issues, including the issue of slavery. In late December 1860, with South Carolina on the verge of secession, Lincoln wrote to two prominent Southerners to affirm the security of slavery and of the people in the Southern states. In a letter to Alexander H. Stephens, whom Lincoln knew from his service in Congress and who later became the vice president of the Confederate States of America, Lincoln asked whether "the people of the South really entertain fears that a Republican administration would, *directly*, or *indirectly*, interfere with their slaves, or with them, about their slaves? If they do, I wish to assure you, as once a friend, and still, I hope, not an enemy, that there is no cause for such fears."[32]

Then, to journalist Duff Green, an avowed supporter since the 1830s of John C. Calhoun's doctrine of nullification, Lincoln affirmed, "I declare that the maintenance inviolate of the rights of the States, and especially the right of each state to order and control its own domestic institutions according to its own judgment exclusively, is essential to that balance of powers on which the perfection, and endurance of our political fabric depends." Green had written to Lincoln in an attempt to secure from him a pledge not to invade Southern states. In his reply, Lincoln turned the tables on Green by pledging that he would not invade the South "only upon the condition that six of the twelve United States Senators for [the seceded states] . . . shall sign their names to what is written on this sheet below my name, and allow the whole to be published together[:] 'We recommend to the people of the States we represent respectively, to suspend all action for dismemberment of the Union, at least, until some act, deemed to be violative of our rights, shall be done by the incoming administration.'"[33]

While affirming that a state controlled the issue of slavery within its borders, Lincoln nonetheless steadfastly denied the ability of a state to secede from the United States. To do so, in fact, would be to repudiate the idea of federalism, which could exist only so long as the nation was united. In a speech at Indianapolis in February 1861, on his way to assume the presidency, Lincoln posed this question to his audience:

> What is the particular sacredness of a State? I speak not of that position which is given to a State in and by the Constitution of the United States, for that all of us agree to—we abide by; but that position assumed, that a State can carry with it out of the Union that which it holds in sacredness by virtue of its connection with the Union. . . . By what principle of original right is it that one-fiftieth or one-nineteenth of a great nation, by calling themselves a State, have the right to break up and ruin that nation as a matter of original principle?[34]

In his first inaugural address, Lincoln made public his promise not to "interfere with the institution of slavery in the States, where it exists," and not to invade Southern states. "Plainly," Lincoln said, "the central idea of secession, is the essence of anarchy. . . . This country, with its institutions, belongs to the people who inhabit it. Whenever they shall grow weary of the existing government, they can exercise their *constitutional* right of amending it, or their *revolutionary* right to dismember or overthrow it."[35]

Lincoln was saying that only a majority can make a revolution. Neither a state acting in isolation from the other states nor people who lived in a minority of the states were capable of dissolving the Union. He developed this thinking further in his address to the special session of Congress on July 4, 1861, which he called to deal with the national crisis following the attack on Fort Sumter. Lincoln contended that in order to hide the fact that a minority was engaging in rebellion against the nation, Confederate leaders had "invented an ingenious sophism . . . that any state of the Union may, *consistently* with the national Constitution, and therefore *lawfully*, and

Lithograph depicting South Carolina riding on a pig, going "whole hog" for "Secession Humbug" (nonsense or deception), and leading other Southern states over a precipice. Neither Jefferson nor Lincoln believed that secession was legally or politically possible. *Currier & Ives, 1861. Library of Congress.*

peacefully, withdraw from the Union, without the consent of the Union, or of any other state. . . . This sophism derives much—perhaps the whole—of its currency, from the assumption, that there is some omnipotent, and sacred supremacy, pertaining to a *State*—to each State of our Federal Union. . . . [W]hence this magical omnipotence of 'State rights' . . . ?"[36]

In fact, Lincoln argued, the states were not created first—as Jefferson argued—but rather came into existence only with the creation of the nation. First, the Declaration of Independence assigned to the former thirteen British colonies the designation of states; second, the Articles of Confederation declared that the union of these states was perpetual; and finally, the Constitution established and reserved under the Tenth Amendment powers and rights of states under the assignment of "[w]hatever concerns the whole . . . to the general government; while, whatever concerns *only* the State, . . . to the State. . . . Whether the National Constitution, in defining boundaries between the two, has applied the principle with exact accuracy, is not to be questioned. We are all bound by that defining, without question."[37]

In Lincoln's mind, therefore, because the union of the states was "older than any of the States; and, in fact, . . . created them," states enjoyed no existence outside of the union of the states. "The States have their *status* IN the Union, and they have no other *legal status*. If they break from this they can only do so against law, and by revolution." As support for this proposition, Lincoln more fully developed an idea that he had broached in the inaugural address: that the American people had created the nation, in 1776 by separating themselves from Great Britain and in 1787 by creating the Constitution. Confederate leaders therefore were usurping the right of the people to control their lives. "It may well be questioned," he argued, "whether there is to-day, a majority of the legally qualified voters of any State, except perhaps South Carolina, in favor of disunion. There is much reason to believe that the Union men are the majority in many, if not every other one, of the so-called seceded states. . . . This is essentially a People's contest. . . . I am most happy to believe that the plain people understand and appreciate this."[38]

From this platform, Lincoln constructed the proposition that popular control of government was an experiment with three parts. The people had successfully *established* government resting on popular consent with the Declaration of Independence and created an *administrative form* for that government with the Constitution. "One [experiment] still remains—its successful *maintenance* against a formidable [internal] attempt to overthrow it. . . . Such will be a great lesson of peace; teaching men that what they cannot take by an election, neither can they take it by a war—teaching all, the folly of being the beginners of a war."[39]

Lincoln consistently emphasized the twin issues of federalism and state rights throughout the war, increasingly sharpening his emphasis on popular control of government and his confidence that the American people wanted the nation to be united once again under the Constitution. Therefore, when, in August 1861, the governor of Kentucky wrote to Lincoln to have Union troops removed from his state, Lincoln countered this request with his belief that, in fact, the *people* of the state wanted the troops (most of whom were Kentuckians) to remain there. In closing his letter, Lincoln expressed disappointment in the governor, especially because the president had searched for and could "not find, in your not very short letter, any declaration, or intimation, that you entertain any desire for the preservation of the Federal Union."[40]

In December 1862, when the western section of Virginia petitioned for statehood, Lincoln further clarified his thinking on these issues. It was argued, he wrote, that in order for a new state to be created out of the old state, the Virginia legislature would have to give its consent. Why, he countered, should the Virginia legislature be involved in the issue, since it was dominated by people who were engaged "in open rebellion against" the United States? "Can this government stand," Lincoln posed, "if it indulges constitutional constructions by which men in open rebellion against it, are to be accounted, man for man, the equals of those who maintain their loyalty to it? ... It is said that the admission of West-Virginia, is secession, and tolerated only because it is our secession. Well, if we call it by that name, there is still difference enough between secession against the constitution, and secession in favor of the constitution."[41]

III

Thomas Jefferson and Abraham Lincoln approached the topic of states' rights or state rights from opposite perspectives. Jefferson feared that the national government would consolidate all powers unto itself and clung to the Tenth Amendment as protecting powers collectively reserved to the states. Lincoln viewed the issue of state rights from the perspective of civil war and worried that the doctrine of nullification threatened the nation's survival. That said, Jefferson and Lincoln also agreed on many points. Each subscribed to the concept of federalism, and they defined it similarly: that the Constitution gave the national government responsibility over issues affecting the general welfare and that a state controlled its local matters. While Jefferson argued that states acting together might nullify a law that Congress passed that exceeded its authority under the Constitution, he did not believe that the right of nullification extended to secession, a belief that Lincoln held even more strongly than Jefferson. Both men labeled secession as promoting anarchy.

Jefferson and Lincoln also believed that the US Constitution had created "a more perfect union" of the people and the states than had existed under the Articles of Confederation, and each subscribed to the idea that sovereignty under the Constitution resided in the people of the United States rather than with the states. Unfortunately, Jefferson's positions became entangled with John C. Calhoun's in the 1830s, and secessionist Southerners twisted his Kentucky Resolutions in order to justify their position.

Most importantly, neither Jefferson nor Lincoln subscribed to the belief that revolutionary change, through a state declaring its singular right to define the meaning of laws or through states acting together, could be accomplished in the nation without a majority supporting it. In the end, therefore, both men placed their hopes in the ability of the democratic process to accommodate the need for change through frequent elections (Jefferson) and the sovereignty of the people through constitutional change (Lincoln) to obviate the need for a state to claim the right of secession.

It is inevitable that individuals will divide on issues and values, and our history shows that no exact demarcation between state and national authority is possible; however, if the Civil War taught any single lesson, it would seem to be that in a republic, the people control government. As Lincoln reminded his countrymen in his first inaugural address, "Unanimity is impossible; the rule of minority, as a permanent arrangement, is wholly inadmissible; so that, rejecting the majority principle, anarchy, or despotism in some form, is all that is left."[42]

"RELIGIOUS OPINIONS OR BELIEF"

Based on his writings in the 1770s and 1780s, Thomas Jefferson had every reason to believe that his religious views would be one of the topics he would have to address as president. He was right. Abraham Lincoln, by way of contrast, likely did not expect that his religious beliefs would be an issue during his presidency. He was wrong.

I

It did not take long as president for Thomas Jefferson to feel the ire of some citizens concerning his religious beliefs. Statements concerning religion appear in his first inaugural address five times. He first broached the subject in the negative context of differing political opinions: "[H]aving banished from our land that religious intolerance under which mankind so long bled and suffered, we have yet gained little if we countenance a political intolerance as despotic, as wicked, and capable of as bitter and bloody persecutions." On November 2, 1801, the *Connecticut Courant* (a Hartford newspaper) published a letter in which the writer took the president to task for this language: "What, Sir, is your meaning, when you state that we have *banished* from our land religious intolerance? When did any religious intolerance exist in our land? . . . If a solitary instance or two of persecution for the sake of religious opinions occurred among the fanatics who first settled the country, surely nothing happened to warrant the imputation contained in this message." A week later, the *Courant* published a follow-up letter from the same writer, who continued his assault on Jefferson's language and sincerity. "In the conclusion of your address, you . . . close with an ejaculation to the 'infinite power that rules the destinies of the universe,' in favor of your councils. If by that power you mean the Supreme God, I heartily unite with you, for we have great and pressing occasion for his assistance."[1]

From the other side of the political scene, a letter from one of Jefferson's supporters was published in March 1801 in the *Boston Independent Chronicle & Universal Advertiser*, saying that whereas Jefferson's enemies had portrayed him "in all the detestable qualities of infidelity, immorality, and atheism[;] . . . as the subverter of religion; the demoralizer, the deist," in fact Jefferson's address proved that he "exhibits the benevolence, candor, and magnanimity of a [C]hristian, patriot, and philosopher." The same writer continued the next week to attribute the denunciations of Jefferson as an atheist to a twisted reading of his writings about religion in *Notes on the State of Virginia*, stemming from "'pulpit, drum ecclesiastic,' from one end of the continent to the other, to degrade the man and to sink him into forgetfulness, as unqualified for a ruler."[2]

Jefferson had anticipated that his statements in *Notes* about religious intolerance in Virginia would not be popular with many readers. Writing to a French correspondent in June 1785, Jefferson confided that he planned carefully to distribute the two hundred copies he had printed in France because "strictures on slavery and on the constitution of Virginia . . . are the parts which I do not wish to have made public, at least, till I know whether their publication would do most harm or good."[3]

One of the greatest flaws that Jefferson identified in the Virginia Constitution of 1776 in Query XVII in *Notes* was the fact that it gave preference to the Church of England over all other faiths. While he acknowledged that the state's constitution repealed all acts of the British Parliament that imposed criminal penalties on religious beliefs contrary to those of the Church of England, he noted that the document left in place common-law restrictions on religious freedom (for example, heresy was defined as a capital offense, punishable by burning) and statutory measures passed by the House of Burgesses, including punishments for denying "the being of a God, or the Trinity, or assert[ing] there are more gods than one, or den[ying] the Christian religion to be true, or the scriptures to be of divine authority." Punishments ranged from withholding the ability to hold any office in the state to inability to sue or act as a "guardian, executor, or administrator," including the severing of a father's right to have custody of his children. "This is a summary view," Jefferson wrote, "of that religious slavery, under which a people have been willing to remain, who have lavished their lives and fortunes for the establishment of their civil freedom. . . . The legitimate powers of government extend to such acts only as are injurious to others. But it does me no injury for my neighbor to say there are twenty gods or no god. It neither picks my pocket nor breaks my leg."[4]

This language reprised what Jefferson wrote ten years earlier as a member of the Virginia House of Delegates in his "Bill for Establishing Religious Freedom (1777 and 1779)": "*Well aware that the opinions and belief of men depend not on their own will, but follow involuntarily the evidence proposed to their minds[,]* . . . Almighty God hath created the mind free, *and manifested his supreme will that free it shall remain by making it altogether insusceptible of restraint.*" In opposition to this desire, "the impious presumption of legislators and rulers, civil as well as ecclesiastical, who, being themselves but fallible and uninspired men, have assumed dominion over the faith of others, setting up their own opinions and modes of thinking as the only true and infallible . . . hath established and maintained false religions over the greatest part of the world and through all time." Affirming that "our civil rights have no dependance on our religious opinions, any more than our opinions in physics or geometry," Jefferson's statute concluded "*that the opinions of men are not the object of civil government, nor under its jurisdiction* [and] . . . that no man shall be compelled to frequent or support any religious worship, place, or ministry whatsoever, nor shall [he] be enforced, restrained, molested, or burthened in his body or goods, nor shall [he] otherwise suffer, on account of his religious opinions or belief; but that all men shall be free to profess, and by argument to maintain, their opinions in matters of religion, and that the same shall in no wise diminish, enlarge, or affect their civil capacities."[5]

Taken together, these passages from *Notes* and Jefferson's statute certainly contain material that many churchgoers would have found to be objectionable. Other portions of *Notes* contain less obvious but potentially even more disturbing language for a conventionally religious Christian. In Query IV, for example, in the context of Virginia's mountains, Jefferson discussed the passage of the Potomac and Shenandoah Rivers through the Blue Ridge Mountains at today's Harpers Ferry, Virginia. "In the moment of their junction they rush together against the mountain, rend it asunder, and pass off to the sea. The first glance of this scene hurries our senses into the opinion, that this earth has been created in time, that the mountains were formed first, that the rivers began to flow afterwards, that in this place particularly [there existed] . . . a war between rivers and mountains, which must have shaken the earth itself to its center."[6] Without directly saying so, Jefferson's account stands in direct opposition to the sequence of events found in the first chapter of the Bible for how the earth came into being. In Genesis, water first covered the land, and God caused dry land to appear only on the third day.

A second example of Jefferson's challenge to biblical accounts of human history in *Notes* occurs in Query VI, which is by far the longest and most structurally complex of all the chapters in the book. Here he discusses the occurrence of petrified sea shells in mountainous areas, including reports of them in the Andes Mountains, "fifteen thousand feet above the level of the ocean." The existence of these shells, he wrote, "is considered by many, both of the learned and unlearned, as a proof of an universal deluge," but such "deluges" that would have covered mountains in Virginia, much less the Andes, "seem out of the laws of nature." Because areas surrounding the Mediterranean Sea might have a different natural history ("It has been often supposed, and is not unlikely, that that sea was once a lake"), Jefferson reckoned that it was "probable some instances of a partial deluge" may have occurred in the region, "which, according to a tradition of the Egyptians and Hebrews, were overflowed about 2300 years before the Christian aera."[7] Jefferson then offered two additional theories to explain the existence of the sea shells on mountains but found them to be equally unsatisfactory and concluded that "we must be contented to acknowledge, that this great phaenomenon is as yet unsolved. Ignorance is preferable to error; and he is less remote from the truth who believes nothing, than he who believes what is wrong."[8]

As president, Jefferson found occasion to reiterate his views that religion was a private matter when he responded to a group of Baptists in Connecticut on January 1, 1802. "Believing with you," he wrote, "that religion is a matter which lies solely between man and his God, that he owes account to none other for his faith or his worship, that the legislative powers of government reach actions only, and not opinions, I contemplate with sovereign reverence [the first amendment to the US Constitution,] which . . . [built] a wall of separation between Church and State." He continued by saying that as president, he would adhere "to this expression of the supreme will of the nation in behalf of the rights of conscience," but in closing the letter, it has been argued that he complicated this dictum with these words: "I reciprocate your kind prayers for the protection and blessing of the common Father and Creator of man."[9]

Why would a man who advocated separating church and state follow this view with the appearance of praying for God's protection and blessing? This question is not easily answered.

Beginning with George Washington, presidents commonly included religious sentiments in their public speeches, including setting aside days of fasting and thanksgiving. John Adams, especially, linked religion and good government and believed that nations as well as individuals were accountable for sins.[10] Similarly, Jefferson used religious images in his speeches as president, including the closing passage from his first inaugural address, where he expressed the hope that "that Infinite Power which rules the destinies of the universe, [may] lead our councils to what is best, and give them a favorable issue for your peace and prosperity." Four years later, Jefferson concluded his second inaugural address with the statement that he would "need . . . the favor of that Being in whose hands we are, who led our forefathers, as Israel of old, from their native land and planted them in a country flowing with all the necessaries and comforts of life" and the supplication "that he will so enlighten the minds of your servants, guide their councils, and prosper their measures that whatsoever they do, shall result in your good, and shall secure to you the peace, friendship, and approbation of all nations."[11]

When he was home at Monticello, Jefferson attended Anglican church services, as did the great majority of Virginians. As president, when he worshipped in public, he typically attended nonsectarian services held in the House of Representatives, where ministers rotated their ceremonial duties. Church services were also held in executive branch buildings, including the Supreme Court chambers, and Jefferson acknowledged that several states (no longer Virginia) gave preference to one denomination over others.[12] "I consider the government of the U S. as interdicted by the Constitution from intermeddling with religious institutions, their doctrines, discipline, or exercises," he wrote in an 1808 letter. "This results not only for the provision that no law shall be made respecting the establishment, or free exercise, of religion, but from that also which reserves to the states the powers not delegated to the U.S." Nonetheless, various individuals advised Jefferson during his presidency to recommend, rather than *prescribe*, days of fasting and prayer. "That is, that I should *indirectly* assume to the U.S. an authority over religious exercises which the Constitution has directly precluded them from.... Fasting & prayer are religious exercises. The enjoining them an act of discipline. Every religious society has a right to determine for itself the times for these exercises, & the objects proper for them, according to their own particular tenets; and this right can never be safer than in their own hands, where the constitution has deposited it." The fact that Presidents Washington and Adams had acted otherwise held no weight with Jefferson. "Be this as it may, every one must act according to the dictates of his own reason, & mine tells me that civil powers alone have been given to the President of the U S. and no authority to direct the religious exercises of his constituents."[13]

Jefferson clarified some of his thinking regarding his personal religious beliefs in an April 1803 letter to Dr. Benjamin Rush, in which he disputed "the anti-Christian system imputed to me by those who know nothing of my opinions." Jefferson wrote that he opposed "the corruptions of Christianity... but not... the genuine precepts of Jesus himself. I am a Christian, in the only sense in which he wished any one to be; sincerely attached to his doctrines, in preference to all others; ascribing to him every *human* excellence; and believing he never claimed any other." In other words, Jefferson admired the ethical teachings of Jesus but noted that Jesus wrote nothing himself, and therefore,

> writing his life and doctrines fell on unlettered and ignorant men; who wrote, too, from memory, and not till long after the transactions had passed.... Hence the doctrines which he really delivered were defective as a whole, and fragments only of what he did deliver have come to us mutilated, misstated, and often unintelligible. They have been still more disfigured by the corruptions of schismatizing followers, who have found an interest in sophisticating and perverting the simple doctrines he taught, by engrafting on them ... mysticisms ..., frittering them into subtleties, and obscuring them with jargon, until they have caused good men to reject the whole in disgust, and to view Jesus himself as an imposter.

Notwithstanding these views, which Jefferson said were "the result of a life of inquiry and reflection," he insisted that as president, "I am ... averse to the communication of my religious tenets to the public; because it would countenance the presumption of those who have endeavoured to draw them before that tribunal, and to seduce public opinion to erect itself into that inquisition over the rights of conscience, which the laws have so justly proscribed."[14]

Reflecting in 1816 on his experiences as president, Jefferson wrote to one of his supporters:

> I have ever thought religion a concern purely between our God and our consciences, for which we were accountable to him, and not to the priests. I never told my own religion, nor scrutinized that of another. I never attempted to make a convert, nor wished to change another's creed. I have ever judged of the religion of others by their lives, ... [f]or it is in our lives, and not from our words, that our religion must be read. By the same test the world must judge me. But this does not satisfy the priesthood. They must have a positive, a declared assent to all their interested absurdities. My opinion is that there would never have been an infidel, if there had never been a priest. The artificial structures they have built on the purest of all moral systems, for the purpose of deriving from it pence and power, revolts those who think for themselves, and who read in that system only what is really there.[15]

Finally, late in his life, Jefferson undertook an abridgment of the New Testament, he told a correspondent in October 1819, in order to abstract "what is really His [Jesus's] from the rubbish in which it is buried, easily distinguished by its lustre from the dross of His biographers, and as separable from that as the diamond from the dunghill."[16] By never publishing his edited Bible, however, he protected his own personal complex religious views and—as he had done as president—separated them from his professional responsibilities. Throughout his life, Jefferson adhered to the belief that individuals should be free from governmental involvement in their religious opinions. He entertained the hope, as he expressed in his letter to the Danbury Baptists, that states like Connecticut would follow the lead of Virginia (under its Statute for Religious Freedom) and the national government (under the First Amendment), and he made these feelings public, but he did not promulgate his privately held religious views.

II

Before he became president, Lincoln's personal religious views would have been a mystery to almost everyone. In 1846, he ran for election to Congress against a Methodist minister and found himself accused of being "an open scoffer at Christianity." In a handbill that he had printed to confront these charges, Lincoln acknowledged that he did not belong to any church but averred that he had "never denied the truth of the Scriptures; . . . [nor] spoken with intentional disrespect of religion in general, or of any denomination of Christians in particular." He asserted, "I do not think I could myself, be brought to support a man for office, whom I knew to be an open enemy of, and scoffer at, religion. . . . I . . . do not think any man has the right thus to insult the feelings, and injure the morals, of the community in which he may live."[17]

Lincoln also said in the handbill, "It is true that in early life I was inclined to believe in what I understand is called the 'Doctrine of Necessity'—that is, that the human mind is impelled to action, or held in rest by some power, over which the mind itself has no control; and I have sometimes (with one, two or three, but never publicly) tried to maintain this opinion in argument." He said he understood that "several of the Christian denominations" held similar ideas, but he then expressed Jefferson's oft-stated perspective on religion, that he would "[leave] the higher matters of eternal consequences, between [a man] and his Maker."[18]

Although he kept his personal religious views to himself prior to 1861, Lincoln, like Jefferson, frequently employed biblical phrases in his speeches. An early example of this rhetorical strategy occurred in January 1838, when he spoke at the Young Men's Lyceum of Springfield, Illinois, on the topic of violent disregard for constitutionally approved statutes and the substitution of what he called "mob law." At the close of his speech, he appealed to his audience that "the proud fabric of freedom" might rest on "the rock" of *general intelligence, sound morality, and in particular, a reverence for the constitution and laws*" of the nation. Then, Lincoln prophesied, "as truly as has been said of the only greater institution, '*the gates of hell shall not prevail against it*'" (a reference to Christ's appointing Peter as the rock of the Church in the Gospel of Matthew). Another example can be found in his July 1858 speech at Chicago, where Lincoln quoted Jesus's admonition, "'As your Father in Heaven is perfect, be ye also perfect.'" Lincoln told his audience that Jesus did not expect human beings to achieve perfection, but instead to set a standard of morality that would be worthy of attaining. In the same way, he said, in the United States the Declaration of Independence established the principle "that all men are created equal, [so] let it be as nearly reached as we can."[19]

In addition to quoting from the Bible, Lincoln invoked God's blessing on himself and the nation in speeches following his election as president. In his farewell address at Springfield on February 11, 1861, for example, Lincoln said, "Without the assistance of that Divine Being, who ever attended [Washington], I cannot succeed. With that assistance I cannot fail. Trusting in Him, who can go with me, and remain with you and be every where for good, let us confidently hope that all will yet be well. To his care commending you, as I hope in your prayers you will commend me, I bid you an affectionate farewell." He spoke at Cincinnati the following day, where he said that he hoped peace and harmony would yet rule over the land; "under the Providence of God, who has never deserted us, . . . we shall again be brethren." The next day, he told the Ohio legislature meeting in Columbus, "[A]ll that all we want is time, patience and a reliance on that God who has never forsaken this people." On February 18, he told the New York legislature at Albany, "I still have confidence that the Almighty, the Maker of the Universe will, through the instrumentality of this great and intelligent people, bring us through this as He has through all the other difficulties of our country." He repeated this theme in the course of his first inaugural address, when he said, "If the Almighty Ruler of nations, with his eternal truth and justice, be on your side of the North, or on yours of the South, that truth, and that justice, will surely prevail, by the judgment of this great tribunal, the American people."[20]

That Lincoln quoted directly from the Bible and asked for God's blessing in speeches leading to the presidency is hardly surprising, given the religiosity of the American people. Historian Mark Noll estimates that at the time of Lincoln's election as president, between one-third and 40 percent of Americans "were formal members of churches," which is a larger percentage than today. Those Americans who belonged to a church overwhelmingly preferred Protestant denominations, which accounted for over 95 percent of the nation's churches. Moreover, the period saw a sharp increase in the number of evangelical churches, "with rapidly accelerating influence from Catholic, Mormon, Adventist, Jewish, and sectarian communities as well," and from these "came persuasive accounts of God, the human condition, and the means for finding reconciliation with God and neighbor. During this period the evangelical churches, and then others, altered the course of American politics because they gave direction, purpose, meaning, and stability to so many American lives. . . . Only because they were so important religiously did the churches also become so important politically."[21]

Although Lincoln quoted scripture and appealed for God's blessing on himself and the nation, he harbored doubts about whether the United States stood in a covenant relationship with God. On one occasion, Lincoln's language conveyed this sense of ambiguity. Addressing the New Jersey Senate in February 1861, on the way to his inauguration, he said, "I am exceedingly anxious that this Union, the Constitution, and the liberties of the people shall be perpetuated in accordance with the original idea for which [the American Revolution] was made, and I shall be most happy indeed if I shall be an humble instrument in the hands of the Almighty, and of this, *his almost chosen people*, for perpetuating the object of that great struggle."[22]

The early years of the war deepened Lincoln's doubts about whether God had taken a side in the conflict. Sometime in late 1862, Lincoln drafted the following private statement: "The will of God prevails. In great contests each party claims to act in accordance with the will of God. Both *may* be, and one *must* be wrong. God can not be *for*, and *against* the same thing at the same time. In the present civil war it is quite possible that God's purpose is something different from the purpose of either party. . . . I am almost ready to say this is probably true—that God wills this contest, and wills that it shall not yet end." He also returned in this meditation to what he had called the "Doctrine of Necessity" in the 1846 handbill by stating that God could use human beings as His instruments to accomplish His will. Indeed, were this the case, the war should not have begun at all: "By his mere quiet power, on the minds of the now contestants, He could either have *saved* or *destroyed* the Union without a human contest. Yet the contest began. And having begun He could give the final victory to either side any day. Yet the contest continues." Lincoln therefore rejected the "Doctrine of Necessity" in favor of human willfulness: the American people wanted the war, and they were reaping the fullness of their desires.[23]

It is important to note that the date on which Lincoln wrote his "Meditation on Divine Will" cannot be ascertained with certainty, because Lincoln wrote it for himself, not for public view. John G. Nicolay and John Hay—the first editors of his papers—dated the document to September 30, but most commentators, including Roy P. Basler and his staff in the 1950s, accepted an earlier date (September 2), coming in the wake of the Second Battle of Bull Run or after Lincoln determined that he would issue the Emancipation

Lincoln's "Meditation on Divine Will." When and under what circumstances he wrote this important document remain controversial. *John Hay
Library, Brown University.*

Proclamation, which he did on September 22.[24] Historian Ronald C. White
Jr. believes Lincoln wrote the "Meditation" on September 2, based on a
firsthand account that Lincoln was suffering "the bitterest anguish" over
the outcome of the battle. "That same day," White writes, "Lincoln put pen
to paper in a private musing."[25]

On September 13, however—a date falling between the battle and the
preliminary Emancipation Proclamation—Lincoln met with Reverend
William W. Patton and Reverend John Dempster, two ministers from
Chicago, who presented the president with a memorial adopted at a meeting

in their city on September 7 urging Lincoln immediately to emancipate slaves in the nation. The only record that exists regarding their meeting with Lincoln comes from the ministers, who on September 21 reported to their group what the president had said to them. The two ministers quoted Lincoln as saying:

> The subject presented in the memorial is one upon which I have thought much for weeks past, and I may even say for months. I am approached with the most opposite opinions and advice, and that by religious men, who are equally certain that they represent the Divine will. I am sure that either the one or the other class is mistaken in that belief, and perhaps in some respects both. I hope it will not be irreverent for me to say that if it is probable that God would reveal his will to others, on a point so connected with my duty, it might be supposed he would reveal it directly to me; for, unless I am more deceived in myself than I often am, it is my earnest desire to know the will of Providence in this matter. *And if I can learn what it is I will do it!* These are not, however, the days of miracles, and I suppose it will be granted that I am not to expect a direct revelation. I must study the plain physical facts of the case, ascertain what is possible and learn what appears to be wise and right.[26]

It is possible that Lincoln wrote the "Meditation" ten days before this visit. The sentence "I am sure that either the one or the other class is mistaken in that belief, and perhaps in some respects both" can be seen as a restatement of the same thought in the "Meditation," where he said that "[i]n great contests each party claims to act in accordance with the will of God. Both *may* be, and one *must* be wrong." The alternative, however, is that Lincoln was still in the process of working through his beliefs about Divine Providence when the ministers arrived and that he wrote the "Meditation" following the meeting as a personal reflection on what he had said, perhaps in a heated moment, as suggested by the italics.[27] Given the fact that Lincoln frequently modified his position on an issue once he mulled its likely consequences more fully, I think it is reasonable to conclude that the meeting with the ministers, rather than the Second Battle of Bull Run, was the catalyst for the "Meditation," which would date it to sometime after September 13 and make it a prelude to the Emancipation Proclamation.

Whatever private doubts Lincoln may have entertained about God's Divine Providence, in public he continued to say that God was supporting the Union war effort. In December 1862, Lincoln began his annual message to Congress with the statement that "while it has not pleased the Almighty to bless us with a return of peace, we can but press on, guided by the best light He gives us, trusting that in His own good time, and wise way, all will yet be well." He devoted much of this speech to trying to convince the members of Congress that compensated emancipation of slaves was the policy most likely to end the war, and he closed with a statement similar to his opening one: "We shall nobly save, or meanly lose, the last best, hope of earth. Other means may succeed; this could not fail. The way is plain, peaceful, generous, just—a way which, if followed, the world will forever applaud, and God must forever bless."[28]

As the Battles of Gettysburg and Vicksburg in July 1863 seemed to shift the tide of the war at least for the moment to Union forces, Lincoln's public linking of God's will and the nation's arms swelled. In a letter to Springfield friend James Conkling in August, Lincoln closed with the statement that although the end of the war did not seem as distant as it once had, people should not be overly optimistic that victory would come quickly. "Let us diligently apply the means, never doubting that a just God, in his own good time, will give us the rightful result." And at the dedication of the national cemetery at Gettysburg in November, he said that the war was being fought in order to reestablish the founding principle of the nation—"that all men are created equal"—and that "under God," the nation would achieve this rebirth of freedom.[29]

He expanded on these religious sentiments as well as the idea that the war was now being fought to end slavery in a letter to Mrs. Horace Mann the following April. He wrote to thank her for sending petitions from youngsters that all slave children might one day be free: "Please tell these little people . . . that, while I have not the power to grant all they ask, I trust they will remember that God has, and that, as it seems, He wills to do it." Also in April, at a gathering in Baltimore to raise money for the relief of wounded soldiers, Lincoln recalled his decision to use African American troops in the war effort, begun with the Emancipation Proclamation, and said he had done so "[u]pon a clear conviction of duty . . . to turn that element of strength to account." He declared, "I am responsible for it to the American people, to the [C]hristian world, to history, and on my final account to God."[30]

On September 4, he wrote to Eliza P. Gurney, an antislavery Quaker who had visited him in October 1862, to thank her for trying "to strengthen my reliance on God." Lincoln continued, "I am much indebted to the good

[C]hristian people of the country for their constant prayers and consola-
tions. . . . [W]e must work earnestly in the best light He gives us, trusting
that so working still conduces to the great ends He ordains. Surely He
intends some great good to follow this mighty convulsion, which no mortal could make, and no mortal could stay." The apex of this progression
occurred in early November 1864, when Lincoln heard that he had been
reelected as president. Addressing a crowd that came to serenade him on
the evening of November 10, Lincoln said, "I am deeply sensible to the high
compliment of a re-election; and duly grateful, as I trust, to Almighty God
for having directed my countrymen to a right conclusion, as I think, for
their own good."[31]

Finally, in the first paragraphs of his second inaugural address, Lincoln
specified the cause of the war—strengthening, perpetuating, and extending
slavery—and intimated that God was using the struggle to end the institution: "American Slavery is one of those offences which, in the providence of
God, must needs come, but which, having continued through His appointed
time, He now wills to remove." Based on this line of thinking and Lincoln's
public statements, it can be argued that Lincoln came to believe that God
was using the Civil War to abolish slavery or, in the words of noted Lincoln
historian David Donald, that this portion of the second inaugural "absolved
both the South and the North of guilt for the never ending bloodshed."[32]

The last half of the second inaugural address, however, challenges this
interpretation. There, Lincoln harked back to his "almost favored nation"
metaphor in his address to the New Jersey Senate and to his "Meditation
on Divine Will." By referring to *American*, rather than *Southern*, slavery,
Lincoln emphasized the fact that the institution had not been confined to
the South and acknowledged that all Americans had "looked for an easier
triumph, and a result less fundamental and astounding. Both read the same
Bible, and pray to the same God; and each invokes His aid against the other.
. . . The prayers of both could not be answered; that of neither has been
answered fully. The Almighty has his own purposes." These words reprise
not only the "Meditation on Divine Will" but also Lincoln's September
1864 letter to Eliza P. Gurney: "The purposes of the Almighty are perfect,
and must prevail, though we erring mortals may fail to accurately perceive
them in advance. We hoped for a happy termination of this terrible war
long before this; but God knows best, and has ruled otherwise. We shall
yet acknowledge His wisdom and our own error therein."[33]

Continuing this theme, Lincoln pointed out to his audience that the war's persistence—even after it became apparent that it would destroy slavery—led him to question any sense of righteousness that either he or Northerners may have felt about their role in ending the institution:

> If we shall suppose that American Slavery . . . having continued through His appointed time, He now wills to remove, and that He gives to both North and South, this terrible war, as the woe due to those by whom the offence came, shall we discern therein any departure from those divine attributes which the believers in a Living God ascribe to Him? Fondly do we hope— fervently do we pray—that this mighty scourge of war may speedily pass away. Yet, if God wills that it continue, until all the wealth piled up by the bond-man's two hundred and fifty years of unrequited toil shall be sunk, and until every drop of blood drawn with the lash, shall be paid by another drawn with the sword, as was said three thousand years ago, so still it must be said "the judgments of the Lord, are true and righteous altogether."[34]

Because of his knowledge that humans lack a perfect understanding of God's will, Lincoln closed his speech with a remarkable statement of magnanimity and hope for the future. We are familiar with his promise of "malice toward none; with charity for all." Less familiar are his closing words that emphasized what people *could* do. Instead of using religion to justify their hatred and making God part of their anger, he said that it was possible for Northerners and Southerners to "achieve *and cherish* a just, and a lasting peace, among ourselves, and with all nations."[35]

III

In expressing the conclusion that God governed human existence, it can be argued that Lincoln separated himself from Jefferson, who—with the exception of the passage in *Notes* where he speculated that God might punish slaveholders for their actions—believed that God did not intervene in human history.[36] If this is the case, Lincoln also violated Jefferson's dictum that the president should remain silent concerning his specific religious beliefs.

On balance, however, this reasoning will not bear scrutiny, because there are more similarities than differences between Thomas Jefferson and Abraham Lincoln concerning how they acted on their religious beliefs. For both men, religion remained an intensely private matter even though each used biblical references and appeals to God in some of their public speeches. Jefferson repeatedly expressed the opinion that government's powers extended to actions only and not to beliefs, and Lincoln's chastening rhetoric in his second inaugural address leads to the same conclusion.

Finally, it must be said that the great majority of Americans in both eras wanted something more from both men. Believers in Jefferson's time feared that as president, he would confiscate their Bibles and outlaw religious observances in the nation, and Northerners expected Lincoln to say in his second inaugural address that God had led him and his people to victory. In this vein, it is imperative to note that Lincoln inferred from early newspaper accounts of his speech that the second inaugural "would not be immediately popular." Ten days after his address, he wrote to journalist and politician Thurlow Weed, "Men are not flattered by being shown that there has been a difference of purpose between the Almighty and them. To deny it, however, in this case, is to deny that there is a God governing the world." And—similarly to Jefferson—Lincoln refused to say that God had led him to this insight. Rather, he said he had learned as president that the war had been too complex and astounding for mortals to comprehend, and this truth humbled him. "It is a truth which I thought needed to be told; and as whatever of humiliation there is in it, falls most directly on myself, I thought others might afford for me to tell it."[37]

Many Americans today continue to believe that the United States is a "Christian nation" and that because it enjoys a covenant relationship with God, the president should lead citizens to that truth. Neither Jefferson nor Lincoln, however, believed that the president—or any mortal—could infer God's will. For Jefferson, the Virginia Statute for Religious Freedom and the First Amendment to the Constitution built "a wall of separation between Church and State." Lincoln concurred when he affirmed that "the Will of God prevails."[38]

Chapter Five

"ACT[S] OF INDEMNITY"

One can hardly turn on the TV or open a newspaper these days without encountering groups of citizens who are intent on defending the Constitution against people whom they view as enemies of that document. Some of these groups have joined forces with a national organization that dubs itself Oath Keepers, headquartered in Las Vegas. The primary purpose of the Oath Keepers, according to the group's website, is to educate citizens about what it means to swear, as members of the armed forces and elected officials—including the president of the United States—do, "to support and defend the Constitution against all enemies, foreign and domestic."[1]

One graphic image circulating on the Internet in this regard depicts Abraham Lincoln on a wanted poster once published by the Council of Conservative Citizens, the descendant of the White Citizens Councils of the 1950s. The poster labels him as "Abraham HONEST ABE Lincoln, 16th President of the United States" and accuses him of being guilty, among other things, of making war in opposition to the US Constitution, having suspended the writ of habeas corpus, and perpetrating "numerous HEINOUS crimes against the SOUTHern States and AMERICANS in general."[2]

Thomas Jefferson is another early president who occasionally comes under fire from historians and political scientists for abrogating provisions of the Constitution by making war against Barbary Coast pirates without congressional authorization (1801–5), illegally acquiring the Louisiana Territory from France (1803), and asserting what has come to be known as "executive privilege" during Aaron Burr's trial for treason (1807). In acquiring the Louisiana Territory by treaty, Jefferson acknowledged in a letter that "the executive . . . have done an act beyond the Constitution" because that document contained "no provision for our holding foreign territory, still less for incorporating foreign nations into our Union." Nevertheless, the president asked Congress to approve his actions, requesting the Senate to give its consent to the treaty by a two-thirds majority and the House of Representatives to appropriate the funds to pay for the purchase. Jefferson justified these recommendations based on his belief that the people of the nation would approve the purchase through an "act of indemnity," an exemption granted to public officers from penalties attaching to unconstitutional or illegal actions, for "doing for them unauthorized, what we know they would have done for themselves had they been in a situation to do it." He went on to explain:

> It is the case of a guardian, investing the money of his ward in purchasing an important adjacent territory; and saying to him when of age, I did this for your good; I pretend no right to bind you: you may disavow me, and I must get out of the scrape as I can: I thought it my duty to risk myself for you. But we shall not be disavowed by the nation, and their act of indemnity will confirm and not weaken the Constitution, by more strongly marking out its lines.[3]

Although President Lincoln did not use Jefferson's words, he repeatedly followed the logic of Jefferson's defense of his actions by asking Congress to grant retroactive ratification ("act[s] of indemnity") for raising troops, implementing a blockade against Southern ports, and suspending the writ of habeas corpus, and Congress obliged. Lincoln also, however, accused Southerners of engaging in "ingenious sophism," superficially plausible but fallacious reasoning, when they offered "self defence" as justification for their attack on Fort Sumter in April 1861.[4]

As we compare the actions of Presidents Jefferson and Lincoln, it is important to refer to the Constitution itself in order to judge which presidential actions may have been constitutionally based. One does not have to be an Oath Keeper to believe that government officials should be held accountable for their actions based on fundamental law, not on what is convenient or politically expedient.

I

Early in his term as secretary of state during George Washington's first administration, Jefferson advocated a "strict construction" of the Constitution. For example, when Alexander Hamilton argued that the "necessary and

23146

Jefferson's letter to Kentucky senator John Breckinridge, which says that the country would grant an "act of indemnity" to the president and Congress for acquiring the Louisiana Territory from France even though the Constitution did not specifically grant the national government such authority. *Thomas Jefferson to John Breckinridge, August 12, 1803. Library of Congress.*

proper" clause of Article I, Section 8, gave Congress the authority to create a national bank, Jefferson countered Hamilton's argument with the belief that the bank was "'merely' convenient," not "necessary"; therefore, Congress had exceeded its specified powers. Reading the Constitution backward from the Tenth Amendment, Jefferson argued that by incorporating a bank, Congress was assuming a power not delegated to it by the Constitution. "To take a single step beyond the boundaries thus specially drawn around the powers of Congress," Jefferson warned, "is to take possession of a boundless field of power, no longer susceptible of any definition."[5]

When Hamilton proposed that Congress pass a protective tariff, a tax on imported goods to make them more expensive than domestic products in order to protect nascent manufacturers in the nation from foreign competition, Jefferson again opposed the legislation because he believed it was unconstitutional. Writing to President Washington in September 1792, Jefferson shared his belief that Hamilton justified the tariff based on the sham argument that it was for the *general welfare* of the nation. Were that the case, Jefferson reasoned, the legislature would have no restraints, "since no government has a legitimate right to do what is not for the welfare of the governed." In short, by sponsoring the national bank and the protective tariff, Hamilton was "subverting step by step the principles of the constitution, which he has so often declared to be a thing of nothing which must be changed."[6] With respect to this last accusation, Jefferson may have been basing his charge on Hamilton's writing in "Federalist #1" about the need for *a government at least equally energetic with the one proposed.*[7]

It is within this context of the Constitution as establishing limits on the powers of the national government that Jefferson's statements in the Kentucky Resolutions (1798) are best understood. When Congress passed the Alien and Sedition Acts during the height of the war scare with France, Jefferson opposed the legislation as an attack on federalism. One of the provisions of the Sedition Act transferred the grand jury power of indictment from state to national authority, and Jefferson viewed this action as unconstitutional because, as he wrote to James Monroe in September 1798, the states "are originally competent to the cognisance of all infractions of the rights of one citizen by another citizen: and they retain all their judiciary cognisances not expressly alienated by the federal constitution." Because the Constitution had not shifted this responsibility from the states to the nation, state authority "is therefore not alienated, but remains under the protection of the [state] courts." In October 1798, Jefferson enclosed in a letter to James Madison a draft "Petition on the Election of Jurors" that he had prepared for the Virginia assembly urging that body "to preserve the trial by jury, in its pure and original spirit, as the true tribunal of the people, for a mitigation in the execution of hard laws . . . and may afford some protection to persecuted man, whether alien or citizen, which the aspect of the times warns we may want."[8]

The final chapter in this episode occurred in August 1799, when Jefferson's fears escalated under the belief that the national government would declare that English common law had been established in the nation at the time of independence and therefore could direct the way courts in the nation should function. Writing to his friend John Taylor, Jefferson asserted that before the American Revolution, "the nation of Virginia had, by the organs they then thought proper to constitute, established a system of laws," including English common law, but nothing of the sort had been done nationally. At that time, however, "there existed no such nation as the United States. . . . So that the common law did not become, *ipso facto* [by the fact itself], law on the new association." Were it so, US courts would have "jurisdiction co-extensive with that law, that is to say, general over all cases and persons," and the state courts "may be shut up, as there then will be nothing to hinder citizens of the same State suing each other in the federal courts in every case."[9]

These experiences with Hamilton in Washington's cabinet and later in Virginia with regard to the authority of national courts carried over to Jefferson's first inaugural address, in which he promised that his administration would "with courage and confidence pursue our own federal and republican principles" and pledged "the support of state governments in all their rights, as the most competent administrations for our domestic concerns and the surest bulwarks against anti-republican tendencies." Immediately following this pledge, Jefferson promised to preserve "the general government in its whole constitutional vigor," but this statement is easily taken out of context. Instead of echoing Hamilton's view that the "necessary and proper" clause supplemented the national government's powers, Jefferson's view was that the Constitution constrained the "vigor" of the national government.[10]

Within a few months of assuming the office of president, Jefferson found his strict constructionist views of the Constitution in need of modification. First, he inherited a situation in which pirates operating out of the port of Tripoli were stopping vessels to extort money for the privilege of trading with nations surrounding the Mediterranean Sea. Under John Adams's administration, Congress had authorized ransoms to be paid to the pirates, but Jefferson concluded that they were making war on American shipping and sent a squadron of vessels to the Mediterranean to protect the nation's right to trade without annoyance. In his first annual message to Congress in December 1801, Jefferson informed the body that when he became president, the nation was at war ("The Bey had already declared war") and acknowledged that he had "sent a small squadron of frigates into the Mediterranean" without congressional approval. "Unauthorized by the constitution, without the sanction of Congress," Jefferson wrote, he had approved defensive retaliations against the vessels of the pirates. "The legislature will doubtless consider whether, by authorizing measures of offence, also, they will place our force on an equal footing with that of its adversaries. I communicate all material information on this subject, that in the exercise of the important function considered by the constitution to the legislature exclusively, their judgment may form itself on a knowledge and consideration of every circumstance of weight." In other words, Jefferson acknowledged that he had acted outside of his powers as president and obliquely asked Congress for a declaration of war; no declaration of war ever occurred, however, although the United States remained at war with the Barbary Coast pirates until 1815.[11]

Jefferson followed a similar pattern of informing Congress after the fact in two other areas early in his presidency: failing to execute laws that Federalist-controlled Congresses had passed for national defense and acquiring the Louisiana Territory. In his first message to Congress in December 1801, he reported that government revenues were increasing and, with peace in Europe returning, he expected a further boost of revenues. He acknowledged that war could halt these increases but cautioned that "sound principles will not justify our taxing the industry of our fellow citizens to accumulate treasure for wars to happen we know not when, and which might not, perhaps, happen but from temptations offered by that treasure." Instead of spending the money that prior Congresses had appropriated based on the expectation that the United States would be again drawn into the European wars, he proposed initiating "a sensible and at the same time a salutary reduction . . . in our habitual expenditures. For this purpose those of the civil Government, the Army, and the Navy will need revisal." Reprising a theme of his inaugural address, he wrote that the national government "is charged with the external and mutual relations only of these States"; therefore, he questioned "whether our organization is not too complicated, too expensive; whether offices and officers have not been multiplied unnecessarily and sometimes injuriously to the service they were meant to promote." As a result, he invited Congress to scrutinize the "great mass of public offices . . . established by law" and abolish many of them. "Nothing shall be wanting on my part," he promised, "to inform as far as in my power the legislative judgment . . . to carry that judgment into faithful execution," and he offered the opinion that "the great body of our citizens will cordially concur in honest and disinterested efforts which have for their object to preserve the General and State Governments in their constitutional form and equilibrium . . . and to reduce expenses to what is necessary for the useful purposes of Government."[12]

Jefferson's second annual message in December 1802 repeated the message that the national and state governments had been given separate responsibilities and contained a pledge "to keep in all things within the pale of our constitutional powers, and cherish the federal union as the only rock of safety." Lest we misunderstand what he meant by the nation's "federal union," Jefferson promised to act within the constitutional limitations of national powers and thereby to "endear to our country-men the true principles of their Constitution and promote an union of sentiment and of action equally auspicious to their happiness and safety."[13]

Regarding Louisiana, when he learned that France had acquired New Orleans from Spain, Jefferson dispatched Robert Livingston to Paris to offer to purchase New Orleans and everything that France owned *east* of the Mississippi River—West Florida (the area around Mobile, Alabama), Jefferson hoped. Livingston found Napoleon Bonaparte eager to sell the city and all of French territory *west* of New Orleans. Jefferson, who had railed against Treasury Secretary Alexander Hamilton's borrowing and taxing schemes under Washington's administration, quickly advised the Senate to ratify the treaty and the House of Representatives to borrow the money necessary to seal the deal. One problem remained, however, and it hinged on Jefferson's promise to interpret the Constitution strictly instead of relying on Article I, Section 8's "implied powers" of Congress to make all laws necessary and proper for the body to execute its duties under the document.

Faced with this predicament, Jefferson opted for speed and expediency. In his letter to Kentucky senator John Breckinridge in August 1803, he asked Congress to "secure a good which would otherwise probably be never again in their power." He further advised Breckinridge that Congress should send to the states a constitutional amendment "approving and confirming an act which the nation had not previously authorized."[14] The Senate gave its assent to the treaty, and the House of Representatives appropriated the money, but neither body recommended to the states that the Constitution be amended to cover the actions of either the president or Congress. Ironically, Chief Justice John Marshall ruled after Jefferson's death in *American Insurance Co. v. Canter* (26 US 511 [1828]) that the purchase was constitutional under the treaty-making clause of the Constitution.

In his annual message of December 1806, Jefferson informed Congress that since it had last convened, the Louisiana Territory needed cavalry. The president might have waited for Congress to reconvene in order to deal with this emergency, but instead he reported to the members, "[So] that the commanding officer might be enabled to act with effect, I have authorized him to call on the governors of Orleans and Mississippi for a corps of 500 volunteer cavalry." At the same time, he asked Congress to amend the Constitution in order to subsidize erection of internal improvements and create a national university for the purpose of promoting education in the sciences (see chapter 6). "I suppose an amendment to the Constitution, by consent of the States, necessary," he wrote, "because the objects now recommended are not among those enumerated in the Constitution, and to which it permits the public moneys to be applied."[15]

Jefferson's responses to two difficult situations he faced during the summer of 1807 also illustrate his changing perspective on executive powers. In June, a British warship attacked the USS *Chesapeake* in waters outside Norfolk, Virginia. Jefferson immediately interpreted the attack as an act of war and took steps to place the nation on a war footing. Beginning in August, he commenced almost daily correspondence with Virginia governor William H. Cabell and pledged the national government's support to cover Virginia's expenses in preparation for a possible British invasion. When Cabell expressed hesitation to go beyond the letter of the law, Jefferson demonstrated that he was willing to use executive powers to their fullest, as he had during his agonizing over the constitutionality of the Louisiana Purchase. "It is our consolation and encouragement that we are serving a just public," he wrote at the end of a long letter full of legal disputations, "who will be indulgent to any error committed honestly, and relating merely to the means of carrying into effect what they have manifestly willed to be a law."[16]

As historian Burton Spivak definitively demonstrates, by the end of August 1807, Jefferson had concluded that war with Great Britain was inevitable. He wrote to Secretary of State James Madison on August 20 that "on the meeting of Congress, we should lay before them everything that has passed to that day, and place them on the same ground of information we are on ourselves. They will then have time to bring their minds to the same state of things with ours, and . . . we shall view it from the same position." On September 3, he informed Secretary of the Navy Robert Smith, "I do not see the probability of receiving from Gr. Britain reparation for the wrong committed on the Chesapeake, and future security for our seamen. . . . [I]n that case, it must bring on a war soon, and if so, it can never be in a better time for us. I look to this therefore as most probably now to take place." In early October, as congressmen began to arrive in the capital, having been called back nearly two months earlier than normal, Jefferson confided to Attorney General Caesar Rodney, "Everything we see and hear leads in my opinion to war."[17]

In his seventh annual message in October 1807, Jefferson reported to Congress that following the attack on the *Chesapeake*, "I immediately by proclamation interdicted our harbors and waters to all British armed vessels . . . and deemed it indispensable to secure a greater provision of those articles of military stores with which our magazines were not sufficiently furnished." Unfortunately, Congress had not been in session, and to have called it back into special session "would have lost occasions which might not be retrieved. I did not hesitate, therefore, to authorize engagements for such supplements to our existing stock as would render it adequate to the emergencies threatening us." Finally, he asked Congress obliquely for "an act of indemnity" for his actions. "I trust that the Legislature," he wrote, "feeling the same anxiety for the safety of our country, so materially advanced by this precaution, will approve, when done, what they would have seen so important to be done if then assembled."[18]

When Secretary of the Treasury Albert Gallatin saw Jefferson's draft of his annual message, he characterized it as "a manifesto issued against the British government on the eve of a war" and expressed doubts about the nation's preparation for war, as did Secretary of the Navy Robert Smith and Secretary of War Henry Dearborn. By November, Jefferson saw that key Republican congressmen also showed little enthusiasm for war and backed away from the plans that he had spent the summer developing. On November 1, he reported to Governor Cabell, "Here we are pacifically inclined, if anything comes which will permit us to follow our inclinations."[19]

One of the primary reasons that Jefferson put the nation on a war foot-ing in the summer and fall of 1807 was his conclusion that the British had timed the attack on the *Chesapeake* to coincide with the treason trial of Aaron Burr occurring in Richmond, Virginia.[20] In his 1806 annual mes-sage to Congress, Jefferson asserted that Burr had led an expedition against Spanish provinces in the West and thereby involved his nation in an act of war. Grand juries in Frankfort, Kentucky, and Mississippi, however, failed to indict Burr for committing acts of treason. When Burr fled to West Florida, he was captured and taken to Richmond for trial because of the president's belief that a successful case could be made there that he had plotted treason in Ohio Territory, which was in Virginia's jurisdiction. At Richmond, however, Jefferson found himself at odds both personally and politically with both Burr and Chief Justice Marshall, in whose district the trial now rested.[21]

In a notable understatement, celebrated Jefferson biographer Merrill Peterson writes that Jefferson involved himself more actively in the trial "than constitutional duty alone seemed to require." More directly, Roger Kennedy concludes that "[w]hen Burr entered the southwest of his mind, Jefferson became unjeffersonian." A system of riders between Washington and Richmond kept the president informed concerning the prosecution of the trial. He directed George Hay, the chief government attorney, to offer a presidential pardon to any conspirator who would testify against Burr and authorized Hay to undertake "any expense necessary" to prosecute the trial. Undoubtedly aware of Jefferson's direct oversight of the case, Burr tried to have Justice Marshall issue an order compelling the president to come to Richmond and be deposed regarding papers that Burr believed would prove his innocence. Instead, Jefferson sent a message back to Marshall declining to appear (he did later send redacted documents), lodging his rationale in the Constitution's separation of powers among the branches of government, a rationale that has come to be known as "executive privilege." "The leading principle of our Constitution," he wrote to Hay, "is the independence of the legislature, executive and judiciary of each other, and none are more jealous of this than the judiciary. But would the executive be independent of the judiciary, if he were subject to the *commands* of the latter, and to imprisonment for his disobedience; if the several courts could bandy him from pillar to post, keep him constantly trudging from north to south and east to west, and withdraw him entirely from his constitutional duties?"[22]

Late in his life, Jefferson further delineated his views on the separation of powers among the branches of the national government by arguing that the Constitution wisely made all the government's departments "independent so that they might check and balance one another." He especially denied the assertion of the Marshall Court under *Marbury v. Madison* (5 US 137 [1803]) that the courts alone had the right to review legislation to decide its constitutionality. "The constitution, on this hypothesis," he wrote in an 1819 letter, "is a mere thing of wax in the hands of the judiciary, which they may twist and shape into any form they please." "The judiciary of the United States is the subtle corps of sappers and miners constantly working under ground to undermine the foundations of our confederated fabric," he wrote to another correspondent in 1820. "They are construing our constitution from co-ordination of a general and special government to a general and supreme one alone.... A judiciary independent of a king or executive alone, is a good thing; but independence of the will of the nation is a solecism, at least in a republican government."[23]

Because he believed that national courts—especially the Supreme Court —were exceeding their powers under Article III of the Constitution, Jefferson persisted to the end of his life in the belief that Congress and the president could rein in judicial activism. He rested this conclusion in the belief that because the Constitution established each branch of the government "truly independent of the others, ... [each] has an equal right to decide for itself what is the meaning of the constitution in the cases submitted to its action; and especially, where it is to act ultimately and without appeal." Jefferson's opinion was not lost on later generations. When he vetoed Congress's rechartering of the second national bank, President Andrew Jackson (advised, ironically, by his attorney general, Roger B. Taney) justified his action with the statement that "Congress, the executive and the court, must each for itself be guided by its own opinion of the Constitution. Each public officer, who takes an oath to support the Constitution, swears that he will support it as he understands it, and not as it is understood by others."[24]

II

From an early point in his political career, Lincoln expressed devotion to the Constitution and the nation's laws. In January 1838, he delivered an address to the Young Men's Lyceum in Springfield, Illinois, where he had recently relocated. His address followed in the wake of the assassination of abolitionist Elijah Lovejoy in Alton, Illinois, the preceding November, and in it Lincoln impressed on his audience the dangers of mob rule. The nation's founders, he said, were gone, and with them, a devotion to the founding principles of the nation in the American Revolution, especially the rule of law. "They *were* the pillars of the temple of liberty;" he told the crowd, "and now, that they have crumbled away, that temple must fall, unless we, their descendants, supply their places with other pillars, hewn from the solid quarry of sober reason." Lincoln warned the audience that whereas a passion for liberty had carried the nation through its founding, that positive emotion was being replaced by "the deep rooted principles of *hate*, and the powerful motive of *revenge*." The only salvation for the nation lay in "a strict observance of all the laws," even those that needed to be changed. "There is no grievance that is a fit object of redress by mob law. . . . Reason, cold, calculating, unimpassioned reason, must furnish all the materials for our future support and defence."[25]

The Supreme Court's ruling in *Dred Scott v. Sandford* (60 US 393 [1857]) tested Lincoln's resolve as he had expressed it in his Lyceum address regarding obedience to constitutional and legal issues. In a speech in June 1857, at Springfield, Lincoln said he and other Republicans offered no resistance to the court's decision. "We believe," he said, "as much as Judge Douglas, (perhaps more) in obedience to, and respect for the judicial department of government. We think its decisions on Constitutional questions, when fully settled, should control, not only the particular cases decided, but the general policy of the country, subject to be disturbed only by amendments of the Constitution as provided in that instrument itself." Believing the decision to be erroneous, however, Lincoln pledged to "do what we can to have it [over-ruled]" because of the court's erroneous—in his mind—basis for its decision in fact and law.[26]

As these statements indicate, Lincoln found himself walking a fine line between respect for the Constitution, laws, and Supreme Court rulings and beliefs that the nation was on the wrong track in moving toward a nation where slavery might become universal. For example, writing to Salmon P. Chase in June 1859, Lincoln took up the issue of the Fugitive Slave Law and challenges to its legality in several Northern states, including movements to nullify the legislation, and a move on the part of some to include in the Republican platform of 1860 a statement calling for its repeal:

I think congress has constitutional authority to enact a
Fugitive Slave law, [but] I have never elaborated an opinion
upon the subject. My view has been, and is, simply this: The
U.S. constitution says the fugitive slave *"shall be delivered
up"* but it does not expressly say who shall deliver him up.
Whatever the constitution says *"shall be done"* and has omitted
saying who shall do it, the government established by that
constitution, *ex vi termini* [from the force of the term], is vested
with the power of doing; and congress is, by the constitution,
expressly empowered to make all laws which shall be necessary
and proper for carrying into execution all powers vested by the
constitution in the government of the United States.

He continued by stating that he had formed this view "on a simple reading
of the constitution; . . . greatly strengthened by the historical fact that the
constitution was adopted, in great part, in order to get a government which
could execute it's own behests . . . ; and the other fact that one of the earliest
congresses, under the constitution, did enact a Fugitive Slave law."[27]

In a speech at New Haven, Connecticut, in early March 1860, Lincoln
argued the opposite side of the issue, that in some instances—failing to
mention slavery specifically in the document, for example—the Constitution lacked specificity. "When men are framing a supreme law and chart
of government, to secure blessings and prosperity to untold generations yet
to come, they use language as short and direct and plain as can be found to
express their meaning," but in the case of slavery, "the Constitution alludes
to [it] three times without mentioning it once! The language used becomes
ambiguous, roundabout, and mystical." Why, he asked rhetorically, did it
not mention slavery directly? Lincoln told his audience he could think of
only one reason: its authors "expected and desired that the system would
come to an end, and meant that when it did, the Constitution should not
show that there ever had been a slave in this good free country of ours!"[28]

As a congressman from Illinois, it was necessary for Lincoln to study
the Constitution's delegation of executive power in Article II in the context of the Mexican War. There were clear partisan reasons for a Whig
congressman to question Democratic president James K. Polk's actions in
January 1846 in sending US troops into disputed territory between Texas,
which had become a state in late December 1845, and Mexico. Significantly,

Lincoln justified his vote against Congress's declaration of war in constitutional rather than political terms. His views on this topic are especially important because they provide a reference point from which to compare his own actions as president during the opening phases of the Civil War. In addition, he had to develop his thinking on this critical question carefully because of intense scrutiny of his actions by his law partner, William H. Herndon. On February 1, 1848, Lincoln wrote to Herndon that the war had been "unnecessarily and unconstitutionally commenced by the President." In this letter, Lincoln also drew the distinction between his negative vote with regard to the declaration of war and subsequent votes "on the questions of supplies [for US troops]. I have always intended, and still intend, to vote supplies." However, he had never approved of the president's conduct in provoking the war.[29]

Two weeks later, Lincoln continued their discussion about constitutional issues related to the conduct of the Mexican War. "Let me . . . state," Lincoln wrote to Herndon, "what I understand to be your position. It is, that if it shall become *necessary, to repel invasion*, the President may, without violation of the Constitution, cross the line, and *invade* the territory of another country; and that whether such *necessity* exists in any given case, the President is to be the *sole* judge." Such an interpretation, Lincoln responded, would authorize the president to decide by himself whether such actions were necessary; in other words, the president would be free "to make war at pleasure. Study to see if you can fix *any limit* to his power in this respect, after you have given him so much as you propose." The Constitution had given Congress the power to declare war, Lincoln counseled Herndon, because kings had always pretended that wars were for the good of the people. "This, our Convention understood to be the most oppressive of all Kingly oppressions; and they resolved to so frame the Constitution that *no one man* should hold the power of bringing this oppression upon us. But your view destroys the whole matter, and places our President where kings have always stood."[30]

When Herndon persisted in probing the voting behavior of Lincoln, as well as the other Whig congressmen, regarding the origins of the Mexican War and its prosecution, Lincoln explained that when news reached Washington "of the commencement of hostilities on the Rio Grande, and of the great peril of Gen: {Zachary] Taylor's army," members of both parties were in favor of "sending them aid, in men and money. It was necessary to pass a bill for

this." Democrats insisted on framing the legislation "with a preamble saying—*Whereas* war exists by the act of Mexico, therefore we send Gen: Taylor men and money." Whigs, however, opposed including the preamble "so
that they could vote to send the men and money, without saying any thing
about how the war commenced," but the Democratic majority prevailed,
"the preamble was retained," and because it was not possible to separate the
preamble from the bill supporting the military, "therefore they voted *for*
both together." Lincoln further developed his thinking on this point in a
speech that he gave in the House on July 27, 1848, when he accused Democrats of being unable to see a "distinction between the cause of the *President*
in beginning the war, and the cause of the *country* after it was begun. . . .
To you the President, and the country, seems to be all one." Whigs, however, not only saw the distinction but asserted that "our friends who have
fought in the war have no difficulty in seeing it also. . . . [Veterans] like all
other whigs here, vote, on the record, that the war was unnecessarily and
unconstitutionally commenced by the President."[31]

Herndon was not the only one of Lincoln's constituents who pressed the
issue with him regarding his views on the unconstitutionality of the war.
When antislavery Baptist missionary John M. Peck wrote to Lincoln that
Polk had acted only when it was apparent that no other options than war
were open for the nation, Lincoln replied that General Taylor and his troops
had—under orders from the president—"marched into a peaceful Mexican
settlement, and frightened the inhabitants away from their homes and their
growing crops. . . . If you *admit* that they are facts, then I shall be obliged
for a reference to any law of language, law of states, law of nations, law of
morals, law of religion,—any law human or divine, in which an authority
can be found for saying those facts constitute '*no aggression*'" on the part of
the administration.[32]

When the Civil War began in April 1861, Congress was not in session.
Without waiting for Congress to reconvene, Lincoln activated state militias,
issued a call for volunteers, spent money to put an army in the field, and
declared an embargo on Southern ports. Lincoln's defense of his actions
before the reconvened Congress on July 4, 1861, sounded at first much like
Jefferson's rationale in the situation with the Barbary Coast pirates: that
the nation was at war due to no action on the government's part except to
defend American lives. "It was with the deepest regret," he wrote, "that the
Executive found the duty of employing the war-power, in defence of the

government, forced upon him. He could but perform this duty, or surrender the existence of the government." And similarly to Jefferson concerning the acquisition of Louisiana, Lincoln appeared to lodge a defense of his actions in a belief that public opinion would vindicate his actions. "These measures," he wrote, "whether strictly legal or not, were ventured upon, under what appeared to be a popular demand, and a public necessity."[33]

These words at first glance would also seem to contradict Lincoln's views in 1848 when he criticized President Polk's actions to provoke a state of war by sending US troops into lands near the Texas border that were claimed by Mexico. What makes Lincoln's actions different from Jefferson's and consistent with his 1848 views, however, is that Lincoln was confident that Congress had the power to make his illegal actions legal. "It is now recommended," he urged, "that you give the *legal means* for making this contest a short, and a decisive one; that you place at the control of the government, for the work, at least four hundred thousand men, and four hundred millions of dollars." Whereas Jefferson argued that Congress should give its consent to the Louisiana Purchase by approving the treaty and appropriating the money because it was good for the nation, Lincoln stressed that it was within the powers of Congress to make the actions of the president legitimate under the Constitution by voting the money necessary to cover his expenditures. Further, far from arguing that he alone was interpreting the document for the good of the nation, Lincoln invited Congress to judge his actions and to sanction them. To be sure, he fully expected to receive endorsement from Congress, since it was controlled by his Republican political party, but the Congress that voted on Jefferson's Louisiana Purchase was equally controlled by his party. The point is that Lincoln asked Congress to agree that his actions were within the language of the Constitution—that he had done nothing as president "beyond the constitutional competency of Congress." "[The president] sincerely hopes," he wrote in closing, "that your views, and your action, may so accord with his, as to assure all faithful citizens, who have been disturbed in their rights, of a certain, and speedy restoration to them, under the Constitution, and the laws. And having thus chosen our course, without guile, and with pure purpose, let us . . . go forward without fear and with manly hearts."[34]

Congress vindicated Lincoln's wishes, and the Supreme Court upheld his actions in the *Prize Cases* (67 US 635 [1862]), declaring that the president "had a right, *jure belli* [the law of war] to institute a blockade of ports in

possession of the States in rebellion which neutrals are bound to regard."
More generally, the court took up the issue of whether the president had
usurped the power to declare war from Congress. Writing for the five-to-
four majority, Justice Robert Cooper Grier ruled, "If it were necessary to
the technical existence of a war that it should have a legislative sanction,
we find it in almost every act passed at the extraordinary session of the
Legislature of 1861, which was wholly employed in enacting laws to enable
the Government to prosecute the war with vigor and efficiency." In fact,
in anticipation of "astute objections" to its actions, Congress passed an act

> "approving, legalizing, and making valid all the acts, proclamations, and orders
> of the President, &c., as if they had been *issued and done under the previous
> express authority* and direction of the Congress of the United States." With-
> out admitting that such an act was necessary under the circumstances, it is
> plain that, if the President had in any manner assumed powers which it was
> necessary should have the authority or sanction of Congress, that, on the well
> known principle of law,"*omnis ratihabitio retrotrahitur et mandato equiparatur*,"
> [the confirmation of an act already performed, or retroactive approval] this
> ratification has operated to perfectly cure the defect.

Finally, Justice Grier drew a distinction between retroactive ratification and
an ex post facto law, which the Constitution specifically prohibited Congress from issuing. "[That] objection . . . might possibly have some weight
on the trial of an indictment in a criminal Court. But precedents from that
source cannot be received as authoritative in a tribunal administering public
and international law."[35]

The most controversial aspect of the president's actions in April 1861 related to his decision to suspend the writ of habeas corpus, first in Maryland
and then in other areas essential to the war effort.[36] In his July 4, 1861, message to Congress, Lincoln acknowledged that "the legality and propriety of
what has been done . . . are questioned; and the attention of the country has
been called to the proposition that one who is sworn to 'take care that the
laws be faithfully executed,' should not himself violate them." He might, he
said, have justified his actions with the argument of expediency, that due to
the Rebellion, "[t]he whole of the laws which were required to be faithfully
executed, were being resisted, and failing of execution, in nearly one-third
of the States. . . . To state the question . . . directly, are all the laws, but one,
to go unexecuted, and the government itself go to pieces, lest that one be

violated? Even in such a case, would not the official oath be broken, if the government should be overthrown, when it was believed that disregarding the single law, would tend to preserve it?" But having asked this rhetorical question, Lincoln affirmed, "It was not believed that any law was violated." He then restated the argument he had developed in his 1859 letter to Salmon Chase, that the wording of the Constitution explicitly covered the current situation: "The provision of the Constitution that 'The privilege of the writ of habeas corpus, shall not be suspended unless when, in cases of rebellion or invasion, the public safety may require it,' is equivalent to a provision—is a provision—that such privilege may be suspended when, in cases of rebellion, or invasion, the public safety *does* require it. It was decided that we have a case of rebellion, and that the public safety does require the qualified suspension of the privilege of the writ which was authorized to be made."[37]

Although he did not explicitly say that the situation respecting his suspension of the writ of habeas corpus was analogous to the issue of whether Congress could pass legislation enforcing the Fugitive Slave Act, he must have believed that it was. The provision of the Constitution under which fugitive slaves were to be given up to their owners appears in Article IV; the language about when habeas corpus might be suspended occurs in Article I. Therefore, disputations in both cases about which branch of the government should enforce the provisions missed the point: "the Constitution itself, is silent as to which, or who, is to exercise the power; and as the provision [suspending habeas corpus] was plainly made for a dangerous emergency, it cannot be believed the framers of the instrument intended, that in every case, the danger should run its course, until Congress could be called together; the very assembling of which might be prevented, as was intended in this case, by the rebellion." This was followed by these important words: "No more extended argument is now offered. . . . Whether there shall be any legislation upon the subject, and if any, what, is submitted entirely to the better judgment of Congress."[38]

Lincoln further justified his actions in a letter to a group of Democrats in New York, who in June 1863 chastised him for illegally suspending the writ of habeas corpus. "Ours is a case of Rebellion . . . in fact, a clear, flagrant, and gigantic case of Rebellion; and the provision of the constitution that 'The previlege of the writ of Habeas Corpus shall not be suspended, unless when in cases of Rebellion or Invasion, the public Safety may require it' is *the* provision which specially applies to our present case." "If I be wrong on this question of constitutional power," he continued, "my error lies in believing that certain proceedings are constitutional when, in cases of rebellion or Invasion, the public Safety requires them, which would not be constitutional when, in absence of rebellion or invasion, the public Safety does not require them—in other words, that the constitution is not in it's application in all respects the same, in cases of Rebellion or invasion, involving the public Safety, as it is in times of profound peace and public security. *The constitution itself makes the distinction.*"[39]

Following this defense of his actions, Lincoln referred to specific examples of men who were "occupying the very highest places in the rebel war service," notably, Generals John C. Breckinridge, Robert E. Lee, Joseph E. Johnston, and others. All of these men, Lincoln wrote, were "within the power of the government since the rebellion began, and were nearly as well known to be traitors then as now. Unquestionably if we had seized and held them, the insurgent cause would be much weaker." To have done so, however, would clearly have violated the Constitution because they had not "then committed any crime defined in the law. Every one of them if arrested would have been discharged on Habeas Corpus, were the writ allowed to operate. In view of these and similar cases, I think the time not unlikely to come when I shall be blamed for having made too few arrests rather than too many."[40]

Finally, Lincoln also deferred to Congress with respect to whether US generals might seize property—including slaves—from Southerners in order to prosecute the war more effectively. Writing in September 1861 to Orville H. Browning, Lincoln said that a general might legitimately seize and use slaves, but not permanently free them. "That must be settled according to laws made by law-makers, and not by military proclamations." To do so, he continued, would be "itself the surrender of the government. Can it be pretended that it is any longer the government of the U.S.—any government of Constitution and laws,—wherein a General, or a President may make permanent rules of property by proclamation? I do not say Congress might pass a law, on the point. . . . I do not say I might not, as a Member of Congress, vote for it. What I object to, is, that I as President shall expressly or impliedly seize and exercise the permanent legislative functions of the government."[41] Again, he did not say that he had developed his thinking on this subject when he criticized President Polk for usurping congressional authority to declare war, but it is reasonable to assume that he did. With respect to the Emancipation Proclamation, it must be recalled that Lincoln issued it under his authority as commander in chief to supplement the nation's military strength, *not to free slaves*, which he believed could be done only through constitutional amendment (see chapter 1).

III

A case can be made that it is impossible to draw meaningful comparisons between Jefferson and Lincoln with regard to the exercise of presidential powers under the Constitution because of the different time periods the two men occupied. When Jefferson assumed the presidency, the Constitution had been in existence for only a dozen years, and during most of the 1790s, he had worked to limit the powers of the national government over the states. The Constitution was seventy-two years old when Lincoln became president, but a question remains regarding the extent to which it had grown in stature during the intervening years. William Lloyd Garrison and other abolitionists openly denigrated the document, and both Southern and Northern politicians used nullification arguments in the era leading to the Civil War.

These arguments notwithstanding, there were important differences between the two men regarding their understanding of the language of the Constitution. As president, Jefferson discarded many of his previous beliefs and acted as a strong executive. At times, specifically with respect to the Barbary Coast pirates, he acknowledged that Congress needed to approve *offensive* operations in the Mediterranean, and he deferred to Congress with respect to fiscal matters. His actions in acquiring Louisiana and during the *Chesapeake* crisis and the Burr trial, however, call into question the extent to which he subscribed to the necessity of the president asking Congress for retroactive ratification for his actions. It is especially telling that he used the term "act of indemnity" within the context of popular opinion, not congressional authorization. If the Constitution, treaties, and laws made under its authority are "the supreme law of the Land," as stated in Article VI, it is impossible for the people—or their elected representatives—to change the wording of the document on a whim. It is also telling that Jefferson wrote to Congress on several occasions that members should initiate the process of amending the Constitution to cover all the exigencies that the nation faced, but he never pressed the issue, including whether Congress had the power to spend money on internal improvements or to create a national university (chapter 6). It is also troubling that Jefferson asserted that because he was the president, he had an independent right to interpret the Constitution.

Although Lincoln never used the term "act of indemnity," it is clear that he understood its meaning and legal standing as allowing—in certain circumstances—for Congress to grant retroactive approval for a president's actions.[42] In contrast to Jefferson, Lincoln acknowledged that when he acted outside the specific language of the Constitution, he did so under the belief that Congress had the power *under the Constitution* to make his illegal actions legal after the fact. His suspension of the writ of habeas corpus remains the most controversial of these actions, but he based his actions on the Constitution's wording, not on his ability to infer its meaning.

Lincoln's words are not only powerfully elegant but also powerfully instructive. When government officials act outside the law—or when groups claim they want to return the nation to constitutional principles—it is important that citizens reach for their pocket copy of the Constitution to validate these arguments.

"SO COMPLICATED A SCIENCE
AS POLITICAL ECONOMY"

Historian Thomas Carlyle characterized economics as the "dismal science"; Irish playwright Bernard Shaw similarly disparaged the field by quipping that if all the economists in the world were laid end to end, they would not reach a conclusion. If there are germs of truth in these aphorisms about economics in general, they may be said to be even more applicable to the study of "political economy," generally understood as the intersection between a nation's economic activities (the production and distribution of goods and services) and its governmental policies under which people acquire property.

Not only does the addition of a political component further complicate the already challenging field of economics, but also it broadens it based on the arguments by Enlightenment scholars that the term must include the concept that a society rests on citizens who work for the general welfare and conform their own welfare and happiness to those of others, referred to generally in early America as "virtuous citizens." In his ground-breaking study *The Elusive Republic: Political Economy in Jeffersonian America*, historian Drew McCoy observes that the founders of the American Republic were steeped in the works of European writers who "seemed obsessed with the idea that a republican polity required popular virtue for its stability and success. Simply stated, [the founders] assumed that a healthy republican government demanded an economic and social order that would encourage the shaping of a virtuous citizenry."[1] But if the founders agreed that creating virtuous citizens was the goal of a proper political economy, McCoy also demonstrates in his book how little agreement existed on *what specific governmental policies* would produce the desired result.

For most of his life, Thomas Jefferson encouraged government leaders to pass laws that favored agriculture over commerce or industry. For example, in *Notes on the State of Virginia* (1787), he wrote that farmers "are the chosen people of God, if ever he had a chosen people, whose breasts he has made his peculiar deposit for substantial and genuine virtue" and that "cultivators of the earth are the most virtuous and independant citizens."[2] Putting words into action, in his first inaugural address in 1801, he promised that one of the "essential principles" of his administration would be "encouragement of agriculture, and of commerce as its handmaid," that is, that commerce would serve agriculture.[3] Following the War of 1812, however, he modified his views because of the problems the nation encountered supplying people's wants and needs during that conflict. In an 1816 letter, he wrote, "[E]xperience has taught me that manufactures are now as necessary to our independence as to our comfort," encouraging "those who quote me as of a different opinion" to "keep pace with me . . . for in so complicated a science as political economy, no one axiom can be laid down as wise and expedient for all times and circumstances."[4]

Half a century later, after substantial economic growth in the nation, Abraham Lincoln promoted the need for both state and national governments to support the development of an infrastructure for linking Southern and Western farms with Eastern markets. Lincoln wholeheartedly subscribed to the components of Henry Clay's American System, wherein funds derived from a protective tariff (a tax on imported goods designed to protect nascent American manufacturers from foreign competition by making the imports more expensive than domestic products) would underwrite the cost of constructing roads, canals, and railroads. Farmers would benefit from these internal improvements by sending their goods to shipping points where they would be collected and shipped to American factories. There they would be converted into products that would be sold internally, thereby creating a unified American market and lessening dependence on foreign (primarily British) imports.[5] As president, Lincoln witnessed the tremendous advantages of the United States in fighting the Civil War resulting from its diversified economy that equipped and supported its armies in the field, and he promoted the need for a transcontinental railroad to link the West with the North and the East.[6]

Although Jefferson and Lincoln lived in different times, each subscribed to the idea that the goal of a successful republican political economy was to promote the people's welfare. A comparison of the views of the two men not only enriches an understanding of the complexities of their views but also deepens an appreciation of the extent to which both men advocated economic policies that fostered the creation of "virtuous citizens." Finally, they agreed that a proper political economy for the nation relied on public support for creating an educated citizenry.

I

Various eighteenth-century European intellectuals wrote on the topic of political economy, including Adam Smith and David Hume, but French philosopher Jean Jacques Rousseau in 1755 produced one of the most compelling essays on the topic, *Discours sur l'Economie politique* ("A Discourse on Political Economy"), which provides a basis from which to understand the ideas of both Jefferson and Lincoln. In the preface to his essay, Rousseau distinguished between *private* economy, governing the actions of individuals and families, and *public* economy ("which," Rousseau wrote, "I call *government*") of nations. He likewise drew a contrast between individuals, who pursue their own needs and desires, and the nation, which pursues the general will of the people. A fundamental component of the government's actions therefore involves pursuing policies that create virtuous citizens.[7]

According to Rousseau, governments have three primary responsibilities. The first is to "[f]ollow in everything the general will" of the people. Although he distinguished between private and public economy, Rousseau believed that both have moral dimensions. He described "the body politic" as "a moral being possessed of a will; and this general will ... is the source of the laws [and] constitutes for all the members of the State, in their relations to one another and to it, the rule of what is just or unjust." According to Rousseau, individuals form societies in order to establish laws that govern their actions in a social setting, and "[i]t is to law alone that men owe justice and liberty. It is this salutary organ of the will of all which establishes, in civil right, the natural equality between men. ... In fact, the first of all the laws is to respect the laws."[8]

In Rousseau's telling, governments exist to guarantee public obedience to laws and to inspire respect for laws: "In this alone the talent of reigning consists." Because good laws flow from the general will, the second responsibility is for government leaders to promote "conformity of the particular wills with the general will, [by establishing] the reign of virtue. . . . It is not only upright men who know how to administer the laws; but at bottom only good men know how to obey them . . . and the more virtue reigns, the less need there is for talent." In this context, Rousseau linked personal security and property with patriotism deriving from the society's laws that promote the general will and bind a nation's rulers to obey the laws. A specific danger in this regard that Rousseau delineated is the tendency for rulers to protect the nation's wealthy individuals and not its poor, thereby destroying a citizen's love of country. Drawing on lessons of history, Rousseau concluded that the greatest evils in nations existed "when there are poor men to be defended, and rich men to be restrained," a situation that occurred most commonly when there were extreme inequalities of wealth.[9]

In order to avoid a society's division into the rich and the poor, Rousseau cautioned governments "to prevent extreme inequalities of fortune," not by taking property from those who have it, even in excess of others, but rather by following certain principles, including not crowding people into small places, but instead distributing them over the nation's territory (he wrote later in his essay, "the richer the city the poorer the country"); not favoring arts "that minister to luxury," but rather "useful and laborious crafts"; not sacrificing agriculture to commerce; and not "[pushing] venality . . . to such an extreme that even public esteem is reckoned at a cash value, and virtue rated at a market price." Nations that divide themselves into opulence and poverty, he warned, destroy the general will by turning citizen against citizen and undermining patriotism. "There can be no patriotism without liberty," he wrote, "no liberty without virtue, no virtue without citizens; create citizens, and you will have everything you need."[10]

To create citizens, Rousseau advised governments to support public education: "To form citizens is not the work of a day; and in order to have men it is necessary to educate them when they are children . . . to regard their individuality only in its relation to the body of the State, and to be aware, so to speak, of their own existence merely as a part of that of the State." Aware that this injunction flew in the face of private education—especially by parents—Rousseau enjoined that "education is of still greater importance to the State than to the fathers. . . . Families dissolve, but the State remains." Public education, therefore, "under regulations prescribed by the government . . . is one of the fundamental rules of legitimate government." Only when children are "imbued with the laws of the State and the precepts of the general will; [and] if they are taught to respect these above all things," will they become adults who value and defend the society that shaped them into citizens. "An individual may be a devout priest, a brave soldier, or a zealous senator, and yet a bad citizen," Rousseau cautioned. "[T]he most general will is always the most just also, and . . . the voice of the people is in fact the voice of God."[11]

Rousseau's third essential duty of government is to provide "for the general wants" by "[keeping] plenty so within [people's] reach that labour is always necessary and never useless for its acquisition." Echoing English common-law principles tracing back to Magna Carta, Rousseau defined "the right of property" as "the most sacred of all the rights of citizenship, and even more important in some respects than liberty itself" because it is "more easily usurped and more difficult to defend than life." When individuals are deprived of their subsistence, in this line of thinking, they become slaves to government, and government can reduce people to slavery by taking away their property. But Rousseau also recognized the need for government to maintain itself in order to secure people's rights, and he cautioned that members of a society must "contribute from their property to [government's] support." Taxes therefore must be within the ability of citizens to pay, but Rousseau also warned against rulers who expand expenditures for their own personal gratification or power or who allow citizens constantly to expand their wants. "From this rule is deduced the most important rule in the administration of finance, which is, to take more pains to guard against needs than to increase revenues . . . ; and perhaps from this comes the common use of the word economy, which means rather the prudent management of what one has than ways of getting what one has not."[12]

Rousseau closed his essay with the caution that a society should curtail a tendency toward accumulating luxuries. He acknowledged that a society might pass laws to prohibit the acquisition of luxuries (for example, barring a wealthy individual from purchasing a fine carriage in which to ride, ornate furniture, or expensive clothing; in short, "multiplicity of objects of luxury, amusement and idleness"), but doing so would infringe on a person's liberty to acquire and manage property and thereby depress productivity. He advised, therefore, that all the people of a nation except the very poorest be required to pay taxes, but only when they are given a say in how taxes are apportioned, and the taxes are proportioned based on a person's ability to pay them. "[W]hy," he asked rhetorically, "should a people oppose the imposition of a tax which falls only on those who desire to pay it? It appears to me certain that everything, which is not proscribed by law, or contrary to morality, and yet may be prohibited by the government, may also be permitted on payment of a certain duty."[13]

II

Although it is debatable whether Thomas Jefferson modeled his ideas of a proper political economy on Rousseau's essay, the overlap between the views of the two men is striking, especially in their belief that agriculture was preferable to manufacturing or commerce in developing virtuous citizens. For example, in *Notes on the State of Virginia* (1787), Jefferson used the word *manufactures* in the title of Query XIX, but the label was a misnomer. "The political oeconomists of Europe," he wrote, "have established it as a principle that every state should endeavour to manufacture for itself: and this principle, like many others, we transfer to America, without calculating the difference of circumstance which should often produce a difference of result." However, he pointed out, "[i]n Europe the lands are either cultivated, or locked up against the cultivator. Manufacture must therefore be resorted to of necessity not of choice, to support the surplus of the people. But we have an immensity of land courting the industry of the husbandman. . . . While we have land to labour . . . for the general operations of manufacture, let our workshops remain in Europe."[14]

In line with Rousseau's bias against cities, Jefferson noted in Query XII, "A notice of the counties, cities, townships, and villages," that because Virginia was "much intersected with navigable waters, and trade brought generally to our doors," Virginia had no townships. Its towns, he wrote, were "more properly [called] villages or hamlets." On occasions, he recalled, representatives in the House of Burgesses had passed "*laws* . . . [that] there shall be towns; but *Nature* has said there shall not, and they remain unworthy of enumeration." Then, in Query XIX, he wrote, "The mobs of great cities add just so much to the support of pure government, as sores do to the strength of the human body."[15] In a letter to James Madison in December 1787, Jefferson offered the opinion that "our governments will remain virtuous for many centuries; as long as they are chiefly agricultural; and this will be as long as there shall be vacant lands in any part of America. When they get piled upon one another in large cities, as in Europe, they will become corrupt as in Europe."[16]

As a further dismissal of the value of manufactures and therefore cities for Virginia in Query XIX, Jefferson reported that the people of Virginia generally made their own necessary articles and exchanged their agricultural products "for finer manufactures than they are able to execute themselves," and he deemed it unwise for Virginians to abandon agriculture for manufacturing. "[G]enerally speaking, the proportion which the aggregate of the other classes of citizens bears in any state to that of its husbandmen, is the proportion of its unsound to its healthy parts, and is a good-enough barometer whereby to measure its degree of corruption." The query concludes with this observation: "It is the manners and spirit of a people which preserve a republic in vigour. A degeneracy in these is a canker which soon eats to the heart of its laws and constitution."[17] Jefferson reprised this paean to agriculture in his first inaugural address in March 1801 by first referring to the United States as "[a] rising nation, spread over a wide and fruitful land" and then expressing his belief that the nation's citizens "[possess] a chosen country, with room enough for our descendants to the thousandth and thousandth generation."[18]

In addition to echoing Rousseau's preference for agriculture over commerce or industry, Jefferson's insistence that a nation's political economy rests on the virtue of its citizens permeates the pages of *Notes*. "Corruption of morals in the mass of cultivators is a phaenomenon of which no age nor nation has furnished an example," he asserted in Query XIX. "Dependance begets subservience and venality, suffocates the germ of virtue, and prepares fit tools for the designs of ambition."[19]

But Jefferson was not oblivious to the fact that Virginia planters had become dependent on trade for items that could not be grown locally, such as sugar, coffee, and tea. He noted in Query XX, on commerce, that over time these luxuries had become "the necessaries of life with the wealthier part of our citizens." Some trade therefore was to be expected, but he advised his countrymen in Query XXII to "leave to others to bring what we shall want, and to carry what we can spare," thereby avoiding wars and the unnecessary expense of "such a navy as the greater nations of Europe possess." Deeming navies "a foolish and wicked waste of the energies of our countrymen," Jefferson observed that it would instead be preferable to "[improve] what they already possess, in making roads, opening rivers, building ports, [and] improving the arts" and that the people—in alignment with Rousseau's essay—would support such ventures with taxes. He calculated that "those who manage well, and use reasonable oeconomy, could pay one and a half percent [on their taxable property], and maintain their houshould comfortably . . . , without aliening any part of their principal."[20] As for the wealthy paying taxes on imported items, Jefferson asserted in his second inaugural address in March 1805 that they paid them "cheerfully" because they could "afford to add foreign luxuries to domestic comforts, being collected on our seaboards and frontiers only, and incorporated with the transactions of our mercantile citizens." As for the farmer, the mechanic, or the laborer, Jefferson boasted that they "[never see] a tax-gatherer of the United States."[21]

In making this boast, Jefferson was fulfilling one of the primary pledges of his first inaugural address: to practice "economy in the public expense, that labor may be lightly burdened" by creating "a wise and frugal government, which . . . shall not take from the mouth of labor the bread it has earned."[22] A lull in the wars between Great Britain and France increased exchanges with those two important trading partners and boosted government revenue. Therefore, in his second annual message to Congress in December 1802, Jefferson gloated that the national government's income was "sufficient for the public wants" and "the produce of the year great beyond example," resulting "from the skill, industry, and order of our citizens, managing their own affairs in their own way and for their own use, unembarrassed by too much regulation, unoppressed by fiscal exactions." Of special interest to the president was the fact that the national debt—which he characterized as "that mortal canker"—continued to shrink as a result of "substituting economy for taxation and in pursuing what is useful for a nation placed as we are, rather than what is practiced by others under different circumstances."[23] A year later, he was able to report to Congress that even adding $13 million to the national debt in order to acquire the Louisiana Territory (Congress had previously authorized paying $2 million for New Orleans alone) had not derailed the administration from paying down the principal and interest on the debt.[24]

III

Preference for agriculture over commerce or manufacturing, suspicion of cities, emphasis on economy in government, and maintenance of taxes within the ability of the people to pay formed the backbone of Jefferson's ideas about the proper political economy for the nation from the 1780s through the majority of his first administration as president; however, in 1804 he changed direction. In Query II in *Notes*, Jefferson had anticipated that a rivalry would develop between the states of Virginia and New York for trade with settlers in the Northwest Territory. Calculating that it was closer by half to Virginia than New York City, and with fewer portages, Jefferson proposed that Virginia finance the construction of a canal to link the Potomac River with the upper waters of the Ohio River, but that plan never materialized.[25] The 1803 legislation creating Ohio as a state provided that a portion of the sale of lands in the state be set aside to fund creation of a national road, and in his annual message in November 1804, Jefferson asked Congress to reflect on "[w]hether the great interests of agriculture, manufactures, commerce, or navigation can within the pale of your constitutional powers be aided in any of their relations," promising, "In these and all other matters which you in your wisdom may propose for the good of the country you may count with assurance on my hearty cooperation and faithful execution."[26]

He expanded on this line of thinking in his second inaugural address as he projected a time in the near future when the national debt would be entirely retired and the Treasury would have a surplus of funds. "[T]he revenue thereby liberated may," he encouraged, " . . . be applied, *in time of peace*, to rivers, canals, roads, arts, manufactures, education, and other great objects within each state." Even war, he envisioned, "will . . . be but a suspension of useful works, and a return to a state of peace, a return to the progress of improvement." Because the Constitution did not specifically authorize Congress to spend money for these beneficial purposes, however, Jefferson proposed that it be amended and encouraged the states to approve such a plan based on the expectation that they would be the beneficiaries "by a just repartition among the states."[27] Congress appropriated money to fund a survey for the National Road in March 1806, and in his sixth annual address in December of that year, Jefferson noted that the Treasury had a surplus and asked Congress once again to consider what other objects the surpluses should be directed toward. "Shall we suppress the impost [tax on imports]," he asked rhetorically, "and give that advantage to foreign over domestic manufactures?" Reprising the theme in *Notes* that the wealthy could and would pay taxes the government collected on luxury items, he philosophized that "[t]heir patriotism would certainly prefer its continuance and application to the great purposes of the public education, roads, rivers, canals, and such other objects of public improvement as it may be thought proper to add to the constitutional enumeration of Federal powers. By these operations new channels of communication will be opened between the States, the lines of separation will disappear, their interests will be identified, and their union cemented by new and indissoluble ties."[28]

Notably, as the nation felt the full effect of the embargo of 1807 during Jefferson's last two years as president, his constitutional scruples concerning whether Congress had the power to appropriate money for internal improvements withered. In his eighth and final annual address in November 1808, Jefferson reported to Congress that the "losses and sacrifices of our citizens" under the embargo had "impelled us to apply a portion of our industry and capital to internal manufactures and improvements. The extent of this conversion is daily increasing, and little doubt remains that the establishments formed and forming will, under the auspices of cheaper materials and subsistence, the freedom of labor from taxation with us, and of protecting duties and prohibitions, become permanent." He acknowledged that the states might want to amend the Constitution to further the "improvement of roads, canals, rivers, education, and the other great foundations of prosperity and union," but he now asserted that such activities fell "under the powers which Congress may already possess."[29]

If it may be said that the negative effects of the embargo on trade changed Jefferson's mind about whether Congress had the power to authorize internal improvements, it is equally the case that the War of 1812 shifted his attention to the need for the nation to expand its manufacturing capabilities. Writing to a correspondent at the end of the war, Jefferson boasted that American "manufactures are now very nearly on a footing with those of England" and reported that machines on a small scale were transforming a family's economy. "Quoting myself as an example, and I am much behind others in this business, my household manufactures are just getting into operation on the scale of a carding machine costing $60 only, which may be worked by a girl of twelve years old."[30] "I have not formerly been an advocate for great manufactories," he wrote to another acquaintance in 1813. "I doubted whether our labor, employed in agriculture, and aided by the spontaneous energies of the earth, would not procure us more than we could make ourselves of other necessaries. But other considerations entering into the question, have settled my doubts."[31]

Living some two decades later, Abraham Lincoln saw early in his life the need for direct government involvement in Illinois to remove barriers to trade. "Time and experience have verified to a demonstration, the public utility of internal improvements," he wrote to Sangamon County voters in 1832 when he first ran for the Illinois state legislature at age twenty-three. While he expressed hope that a railroad might one day connect Springfield with locations in the East, he doubted that sufficient funds might be raised to bring it into existence quickly. Therefore, he placed his hope in improving navigation on the Sangamon River by removing trees that obstructed barge travel, thus quickening the flow of the river in the main channel. He promised that "if elected," he would support "any measure in the legislature having this for its object, which may appear judicious."[32]

Lincoln was not elected to the legislature until 1834, but once there he quickly established himself as one of the chief spokesmen in favor of public expansion of internal improvements. In January 1839, he supported legislation to set aside a portion of the money received from the sale of public lands for building a railroad. His report concerning this issue touted the fertility of the soil of Illinois and its suitability for cultivation, "with the capacity of sustaining a greater amount of agricultural wealth and population than any other equal extent of territory in the world." All that stood in the way of accomplishing such a goal, the report concluded, was to support the expansion of the state's internal improvements "as speedily as possible" in order to move produce from fields to markets. Lincoln proposed to pay for these advances by borrowing money for their creation against the sale of public lands.[33]

When the legislature failed to adopt such a plan, Lincoln supported subsequent attempts to entice railroad developers into the state by passing acts of incorporation, and he helped author a report in 1847 encouraging local residents to buy stock in railroad development. The report conceded that Eastern investors would supply the bulk of the money to build a railroad into Springfield, but it warned that these investors would want to see "something of our own in the enterprise, to convince them that we believe it will succeed, and to place ourselves between them and subsequent unfavorable legislation, which, it is supposed, they very much dread." It also contained the expectation that opening such a railroad would lead to further advancements "and so become, not merely a local improvement, but a link in one of a great national character, retaining all of its local benefits, and superadding many from its general connection."[34]

The argument that governments should support only projects that contributed to the *general welfare* was not unique to the Illinois legislature, as Lincoln discovered when he took his seat in the US Congress. In June 1848, Lincoln added his voice to discussions surrounding legislation to expand internal improvements by arguing that such investments were never merely local in their benefits. "Nothing is so *local* as to not be of some *general* benefit," he argued. "But suppose, after all, there should be some degree of inequality. Inequality is certainly never to be embraced for it's own sake; but is every good thing to be discarded, which may be inseparably connected with some degree of it? If so, we must discard all government. . . . Almost every thing, especially, of governmental policy, is an inseparable compound of the two; so that our best judgment of the preponderance between them is continually demanded."[35]

Lincoln's unwavering support for a protective tariff to increase the cost of imported goods that competed with American products may be only partially explained by the fact that the money raised from the tax would be invested in support of internal improvements. As he prepared for debates in Congress over whether to continue the tariff, he rested the issue more broadly on his belief that the government should do all in its power "[t]o [secure] to each labourer the whole product of his labour, or nearly as possible." According to Lincoln, human behavior could be grouped "into three great classes—*useful* labour, *useless* labour and *idleness*. Of these the first only is meritorious; and to it all the products of labour rightfully belong." Iron, cotton, wool, and many other products, he reckoned, "can be produced, in sufficient abundance, [and] with as little labour, in the United States, as any where else in the world; therefore, all labour done in bringing [these products] from a foreign country to the United States, is useless labour."[36]

As historian Richard Hofstadter noted over sixty years ago, most of Lincoln's public speeches contained a strong prolabor message, beginning with his time in Congress, and it formed the nucleus of his attack on slavery.[37] "We know," Lincoln said in 1859, "Southern men declare that their slaves are better off than hired laborers amongst us. How little they *know*, whereof they *speak*! . . . Free labor has the inspiration of hope; pure slavery has no hope."[38] Lincoln subscribed wholeheartedly to what has been termed "the Horatio Alger theory of labor," the belief that through hard work and a commitment to self-improvement, a person could rise from a dependent situation as a "laborer" to an independent situation of "owner"—the owner of property, to be sure, but more important, of themselves. Speaking at an agricultural fair in Wisconsin in 1859, Lincoln told his audience that if laborers were not able to improve their condition, it would have been better to have been born "a blind horse upon a tread-mill . . . all the better for being blind, that he could not tread out of place, or kick understandingly. According to that theory, the education of laborers, is not only useless, but pernicious, and dangerous. . . . A Yankee who could invent a strong *handed* man without a head would receive the everlasting gratitude" of some people.[39]

As this quotation indicates, Lincoln used the agricultural fair not only to tout the virtues of labor but also to develop broad-ranging ideas about education within the framework of farming. It is well known that Lincoln was self-taught, and it seems reasonable to assume that he formed at least some of his ideas about the farmer's need to improve his life through education by working on his father's farm. As a lad, Lincoln disliked farm work, and neighbors criticized him for all the reading and thinking that he did, which made him appear in their eyes to be lazy. In an autobiographical sketch written for the 1860 presidential campaign, Lincoln estimated "that the agregate of all his schooling did not amount to one year. . . . What he has by the way of education, he has picked up. . . . He regrets his want of education, and does what he can to supply the want."[40]

In 1832, candidate Lincoln shared with his future constituents his belief that education was "the most important subject which we as a people can be engaged in. That every man may receive at least, a moderate education, and thereby be enabled to read the histories of his own and other countries, by which he may duly appreciate the value of our free institutions, appears to be an object of vital importance."[41] As Lincoln learned more about himself and the world around him, he found a mentor for his views in Kentuckian Henry Clay. In the eulogy that Lincoln delivered for Clay on July 6, 1852, he said, "Mr. Clay's education, to the end of his life, was comparatively limited . . . , [but] teaches at least one profitable lesson; it teaches that in this country, one can scarcely be so poor, but that, if he *will* he *can* acquire sufficient education to get through the world respectably." According to Lincoln, Clay devoted his public service to the "advancement, prosperity and glory" of his countrymen. "He desired the prosperity of his countrymen partly because they were his countrymen, but chiefly to show to the world that freemen could be prosperous."[42]

In his speech at the agricultural fair, Lincoln advocated any means of technological improvement that would increase the prosperity of farmers. Mechanization promoted what Lincoln called "thorough cultivation," which he described as "putting the soil to the top of its capacity—producing the largest crop possible from a given quantity of ground." Key to this improvement was education—especially scientific education—in order for farmers to work harder and more efficiently. "[N]o other occupation," Lincoln told his audience, "opens so wide a field for the profitable and agreeable combination of labor with *cultivated thought*, as agriculture. . . . Every blade of grass is a study. . . . And not grass alone; but soils, seeds, and seasons—hedges, ditches, and fences, draining, droughts, and irrigation—plowing, hoeing, and harrowing—reaping, mowing, and threshing— . . . hogs, horses, and cattle—sheep, goats, and poultry—trees, shrubs, fruits, plants, and flowers—the thousand things of which these are specimens—each a world of study within itself." Integral to promoting "cultivated thought" was what Lincoln referred to as "book-learning"—to see what had already been discovered so that a person could pose unsolved problems not yet imagined, by studying botany, chemistry, and what he called the "mechanical branches of Natural Philosophy . . . especially in reference to implements and engineering."[43]

As president, Lincoln put many of the ideas that he expressed in Wisconsin into practice. In his annual message to Congress in December 1861, he observed, "Agriculture, confessedly the largest interest of the nation, has, not a department, nor a bureau, but a clerkship only, assigned to it in the government. While it is fortunate that this great interest is so independent in its nature as to not have demanded and extorted more from the government, I respectfully ask Congress to consider whether something more cannot be given voluntarily with general advantage."[44] Congress passed and Lincoln signed the bill establishing the Department of Agriculture in May 1862, and two years later in his annual message to Congress, he observed, "The Agricultural Department, under the supervision of its present energetic and faithful head, is rapidly commending itself to the great and vital interest it was created to advance. It is peculiarly the people's department, in which they feel more directly concerned than in any other. I commend it to the continued attention and fostering of Congress."[45]

Two other acts that Lincoln signed as president deserve mentioning in this context. In July 1862, he signed into law the Morrill Land Grant Act, the purpose of which was to provide grants of land to the states, turning over thirty thousand acres of public land for each senator and representative, for the "support, and maintenance of at least one college where the leading object shall be, *without excluding other scientific and classical studies and including military tactics,* to teach such branches of learning as are related to agriculture and the mechanic arts . . . in order to promote the liberal and practical education of the industrial classes on the several pursuits and professions in life." This act was sponsored in Congress by Vermont representative Justin Smith Morrill, the son of a blacksmith, who wanted to make a college education available at low cost to anyone who desired one.[46]

Although Morrill's name is attached to the act, it was the brainchild of Jonathan Baldwin Turner, a graduate of Yale and a professor at Illinois College, who believed that people would be better served by studying agricultural and mechanical (A&M) subjects in college than by focusing on classical studies, as was most common in the colleges of the day. Turner knew Lincoln and Stephen A. Douglas, and both men promised to sign legislation creating A&M colleges if they were elected president. Lest we jump to the false conclusion that any president would have done so, it is important to note that Morrill's bill was passed by Congress in 1859, only to be vetoed by Democratic president James Buchanan, who believed that creating colleges was a state or private responsibility and that agriculture and mechanics were not fields suitable for college degrees. Lincoln, however, thought otherwise and signed the bill.[47]

Speaking at the Massachusetts Agricultural College in 1887, twenty-five years after the passage of the act that bore his name, Justin Smith Morrill said:

> The land-grant colleges were founded on the idea that a higher and broader education should be placed . . . where a much larger and broader number of people need wider educational advantages, and impatiently await their possession. . . . It would be a mistake to suppose it was intended that every student should become either a farmer or a mechanic when the design comprehended not only instruction for those who may hold the plow or follow a trade, but such instruction as any person might need . . . and without the exclusion of those who might prefer to adhere to the classics.

The following year, Morrill addressed the Vermont legislature and said, with regard to these colleges, "Obviously not manual, but intellectual instruction was the paramount object. . . . The Act of 1862 proposed a system of broad education by colleges, not limited to a superficial and dwarfed training, such as might be supplied by a foreman of a workshop or by a foreman of an experimental farm. If any would have only a school with equal scraps of labor and of instruction, *or something other than a college,* they would not obey the national law."[48]

IV

Establishing a system of public education in Virginia was one of Thomas Jefferson's primary goals. As a member of the Virginia House of Delegates from 1776 to 1779, he proposed various bills for improving life in his "country," including a plan for universal public education. He delineated his ideas in Query XIV of *Notes*, where he proposed dividing Virginia's counties into five- or six-mile-square sections ("hundreds"), in which the inhabitants would establish a school and hire a tutor to teach their children "reading, writing, and arithmetic . . . three years gratis, and as much longer as they please, paying for it." From these children, one boy would be chosen annually to be sent to one of twenty grammar schools located in various parts of the state; after six years, half of these young men would then be sent for three years to study "such sciences as they shall chuse," at the College of William and Mary. "The general objects of this law," Jefferson wrote, "are to provide an education adapted to the years, to the capacity, and the condition of every one, and directed to their freedom and happiness."[49]

At every stage, Jefferson's plan focused on creating *citizens* who would over time transform life in the Old Dominion. "Above all things," he wrote to Madison contemporaneously with the publication of *Notes* in 1787, "I hope the education of the common people will be attended to; convinced that on their good sense we may rely with the most security for the preservation of a due degree of liberty." Whereas most of the private schools in the state—including the one that Jefferson attended as a young man, run by the Reverend James Maury—taught children from the Bible, Jefferson proposed that the curriculum of the schools in the hundreds would focus instead on having students learn "the most useful facts from Grecian, Roman, European, and American history"; Greek and Latin; and "[t]he first elements of morality." In Jefferson's thinking, young minds were "not sufficiently matured for religious inquiries," but historical examples "will qualify them as judges of the actions and designs of men [and] will enable them to know ambition under every disguise it may assume; and knowing it, to defeat its views." Learning Greek and Latin would form the basis for future study, not of the Bible but rather as "instrument[s] for the attainment of science." Finally, moral instruction would "teach them how to work out their own greatest happiness, by shewing them that it . . . is always the result of a good conscience, good health, occupation, and freedom in all just pursuits."[50]

The full measure of Jefferson's reformist impulses can be found in Query XVIII, on customs and manners, where he addressed the very first instruction that Virginia's children received in the homes of slave owners. "The whole commerce between master and slave," Jefferson cautioned, "is a perpetual exercise of the most boisterous passions, the most unremitting despotism on the one part, and degrading submissions on the other. Our children see this, and learn to imitate it; for man is an imitative animal. This quality is the germ of all education in him. From his cradle to his grave he is learning to do what he sees others do. . . . The man must be a prodigy who can retain his manners and morals undepraved by such circumstances." Reforming education, in other words, marked only the first phase of a system designed to produce fundamental changes in government in the state. Late in his life, he was still pushing the same theme. "Time and reflection," he wrote in 1816, only further strengthened his dedication to reforming society by creating locally based and supported elementary schools. "My partiality for [wards] is not founded in views of education solely, but infinitely more as the means of a better administration of government, and the eternal preservation of its republican principles."[51]

Although Jefferson's gentry peers rejected his ideas of universal education, in retirement he did succeed in creating a new state university—the University of Virginia—and this project marked the culmination of his thinking on education specifically and political economy generally. In a report Jefferson authored in 1818, he once again outlined a system of publicly sponsored education in the state, beginning with elementary schools and culminating with college. Although he did not revisit the specifics of his proposal in *Notes* for creating wards, Jefferson envisioned "primary instruction" as providing "every [male] citizen" with the rudimentary elements of mathematics, reading, and writing to transact business and "to express and preserve his ideas, his contracts and accounts, in writing; [and t]o improve, by reading, his morals and faculties." Beyond these elementary skills, these schools would cultivate an understanding of "his duties to his neighbors and country, and to discharge with competence the functions confided to him by either; . . . [a]nd, in general, to observe with intelligence and faithfulness all the social relations under which he shall be placed." Higher education would continue the citizenship process to "develop the reasoning faculties of our youth, enlarge their minds, cultivate their morals, and instill into them the precepts of virtue and order; . . . [a]nd, generally, to form them to

University of Virginia Rotunda, circa 1933. Jefferson designed the architecture and curriculum for the University of Virginia. *Historic American Buildings Survey/Historic American Engineering Record/Historic American Landscapes Survey, Library of Congress.*

habits of reflection and correct action, rendering them examples of virtue to others, and of happiness within themselves."[52]

In Jefferson's mind, creating the University of Virginia was necessary because he believed the College of William and Mary, his alma mater, was rapidly declining in stature because it was too closely wedded to "English books, English prejudices, [and] English manners." In erecting a curriculum that was heavy on the physical sciences mixed with moral philosophy and ancient and modern languages, Jefferson wanted the students at his university to learn to form conclusions about the world, as he had, based on observation and not from the opinions or beliefs of others. As a measure of how far his thinking had evolved since he wrote *Notes*, in his 1818 report, Jefferson expressed his hopes that his university would "harmonize and promote the interests of agriculture, manufactures and commerce, and by well informed views of political economy to give a free scope to the public industry. . . . [T]he advantages of well-directed education, moral, political, and economical, are truly above all estimate. Education generates habits of application, of order, and the love of virtue; and controls, by the force of habit, any innate obliquities in our moral organization."[53]

V

In the concluding chapter of *The Elusive Republic*, Drew McCoy argues that after 1819, Jefferson reverted to a "rigid, uncompromising agrarian-mindedness" as providing the material basis for the nation's political economy and makes the point that Andrew Jackson prolonged Jefferson's vision by "preventing the implementation of any form of [Henry Clay's] American System."[54] Accordingly, one could easily portray Lincoln as the polar opposite of Jefferson because President Lincoln greatly expanded the role of the national government in promoting internal improvements, industrial expansion, and political consolidation. Using Rousseau's *Discourse* as a reference point for understanding the term "political economy," however, leads to a different conclusion—that, on balance, the two men had more similarities than differences in this area, for three reasons.

First, both Jefferson and Lincoln saw labor, not capital, as the basis of wealth and formed their ideas regarding the proper role of government in promoting economic growth as encouraging people to engage in what Lincoln termed "*useful* labour." Jefferson worried that slavery was destroying a person's willingness to work; "[t]his is so true," Jefferson wrote in Query XVIII in *Notes*, "that of the proprietors of slaves a very small proportion indeed are ever seen to labour." He envisioned a time when his country, and later his nation, would be composed of small farmers toiling for the benefit of themselves and their families.[55] Lincoln expressed similar thoughts in his first annual message to Congress in December 1861. "In most of the southern States," he wrote, "a majority of the whole people of all colors are neither slaves nor masters; while in the northern a large majority are neither hirers nor hired. Men with their families . . . work for themselves, on their farms, in their houses, and in their shops, taking the whole product to themselves, and asking no favors of capital on the one hand, nor of hired laborers or slaves on the other."[56]

Second, both men understood—as Rousseau did—that the measure of whether a nation had a viable political economy rested not in its material wealth, but rather in whether it fostered the development of "virtuous citizens." For Rousseau, Jefferson, and Lincoln, virtue resided in individuals but manifested in actions for others. Rousseau referred to this public-spiritedness as acting for "the general will"; Jefferson conceived of it in terms of "natural rights, convinced [a man] has no natural right in opposition to his social duties"; and Lincoln expressed "a patient confidence in the ultimate justice of the people." The central idea is the same in each case: people achieve virtue when they practice citizenship.[57]

Finally, Rousseau, Jefferson, and Lincoln believed that the best hope for a nation to create virtuous citizens was through public support for education. It is an unfortunate condition of today's society that such discussions, when they occur, often degenerate into an either-or proposition as to whether private individuals or organizations (the family or churches) are better suited to this task. Instead, a more difficult, but ultimately more productive, dialogue would address government's legitimate role in the educational enterprise. Jefferson believed that only public institutions were capable of supporting scientific education because "the buildings and apparatus belonging to each [science], are far beyond the reach of individual means, and must either derive [their] existence from public patronage, or not exist at all."[58] Lincoln referred to public education as producing "cultivated thought" and signed legislation creating institutions specializing in agricultural and mechanical subjects "without excluding other scientific and classical studies."[59]

Near the end of his speech at the Wisconsin agricultural fair, Lincoln said, "No community whose every member possesses [cultivated thought], can ever be the victim of oppression in any of its forms. Such community will be alike independent of crowned kings, money-kings, and land-kings." Although this last reference to "land-kings" was likely a jab at Southern slaveholders, the sentiment is one that Jefferson would have understood and applauded. "Every government degenerates when trusted to the rulers of the people alone," he wrote in *Notes*. "The people themselves therefore are its only safe depositories. And to render even them safe their minds must be improved to a certain degree. . . . The influence over government must be shared among all the people." The ideal political economy, in other words, must include public education so that the people will know that one of their fundamental rights as human beings is to exercise control over government, or—in Lincoln's words—to ensure that "government of the people, by the people, for the people, shall not perish from the earth."[60]

JEFFERSON, LINCOLN, AND THE
IMPORTANCE OF PLACE

Both Thomas Jefferson and Abraham Lincoln were acutely attuned to the importance of place in situating themselves within their physical and social environments. Throughout his life, Jefferson's primary reference point was a specific space: his "country," Virginia. He especially boasted that the climate of the Old Dominion made it a favored spot on earth, and Monticello, in particular, was where he felt most at home.

Illinois touts itself today as "the land of Lincoln," and living in Sangamon County was certainly a step up for Lincoln from working on his father's farms in Indiana and Illinois. But Sangamon County offered Lincoln not so much an ideal physical place as the first social setting in which to cultivate his ability to relate to people, which he developed further when he moved to New Salem, Illinois. This pattern persisted as Lincoln widened his circles of people, rather than harking back to memories of any single location where he grew to adulthood.

The perspectives Jefferson and Lincoln developed toward place provide a vantage point from which to compare the two men and assess their legacies. Both men tried to foster change, Jefferson in his "country" and Lincoln in his nation. Ultimately, Lincoln was more successful in his goal than Jefferson, because they understood place differently. Put succinctly, for Jefferson *place* defined *a people*. For Lincoln, *people* defined *a place*.

I

Wherever he traveled, Thomas Jefferson took the opportunity to compare his new location with the climate and customs of Virginia. As minister to

France in the 1780s, for example, he invited James Monroe to visit him in Paris but cautioned that "[t]he pleasure of the trip will be less than you expect but the utility greater. It will make you adore your own country [read here, Virginia], it's soil, it's climate, it's equality, liberty, laws, people and manners. My god! How little do my countrymen know what precious blessings they are in possession of, and which no other people on earth enjoy."[1] Jefferson continued this theme in a letter to a German prince in September 1785, when he wrote, "I am now of an age which does not easily accomodate itself to new manners and new modes of living: and I am savage enough to prefer the woods, the wilds, and the independance of Monticello, to all the brilliant pleasures of this gay capital. I shall therefore rejoin myself to my native country with new attachments, with exaggerated esteem for it's advantages, for tho' there is less wealth there, there is more freedom, more ease and less misery."[2]

As this letter indicates, during Jefferson's time in Paris, his attachment grew for the place in Virginia that he valued over all others—his mountaintop home, Monticello. He began designing Monticello and having it built in 1770, when fire destroyed the family home, Shadwell. A telling example of his attachment to Monticello may be found in his famous "head and heart" letter to Maria Cosway, a landscape artist whom he met in Paris in the summer of 1786. Jefferson fantasized in that letter that Maria's husband, Richard, might die and that she would come to the United States. In addition to Niagara Falls, the Natural Bridge in Virginia, and other feats of nature, Jefferson hoped she would paint scenes at "our own dear Monticello." "[W]here," he asked rhetorically, "has nature spread so rich a mantle under the eye? mountains, forests, rocks, rivers. With what majesty do we there ride above the storms! How sublime to look down into the workhouse of nature, to see her clouds, hail, snow, rain, thunder, all fabricated at our feet! And the glorious Sun, when rising as out of a distant water, just gilding the tops of the mountains, and giving life to all nature!"[3]

In May 1791, Jefferson had occasion to travel with James Madison to upstate New York and New England. Under the public cover of studying the effect of the Hessian fly on wheat grown in the region, the two men met with prominent politicians to plan their break with the policies of the Washington administration directed by Alexander Hamilton. Writing to his daughter Martha while he sailed on Lake Champlain, Jefferson offered this opinion:

On the whole I find nothing anywhere else in point of climate
which Virginia need envy to any part of the world. Here
they are locked up in ice and snow for 6. months. Spring and
autumn which make a paradise of our country are rigorous
with them, and a tropical summer breaks on them all at once.
When we consider how much climate contributes to the
happiness of our cond[itio]n, by the fine sensation it excites,
and the productions it is the parent of, we have reason to value
highly the accident of birth in such a one as that of Virginia.[4]

Despite all of these positive qualities associated with climate, however,
Jefferson also linked many of his countrymen's negative behaviors to envi-
ronmental factors. Following a trip to Virginia by a French noble in 1785,
Jefferson praised the visitor for the many good things he had written about
Virginians, as well as for pointing to certain character flaws. "I have studied
their character with attention," he wrote. "I have thought them, as you have
found them, aristocratical, pompous, clannish, indolent, [and] hospitable,
and I should have added, disinterested, but you say attached to their interest. This is the only trait in their character wherein our observations differ."
By "disinterested," Jefferson meant that Virginians were "so thoughtless in
their expences and in all their transactions of business that I had placed it
among the vices of their character." Jefferson ascribed this character flaw
"to that warmth of their climate which unnerves and unmans both body
and mind." Comparing traits of Northerners and Southerners based on
climate, Jefferson found Northerners to be "cool sober laborious persevering
independant jealous of their own liberties, and just to those of others interested chicaning superstitious and hypocritical in their religion," whereas
Southerners were "fiery Voluptuary indolent unsteady independant zealous
for their own liberties, but trampling on those of others [read here, slavery]
generous candid without attachment or pretentions to any religion but that
of the heart. These characteristics grow weaker and weaker by gradation
from North to South and South to North, insomuch that an observing
traveler, without the aid of the quadrant may always know his latitude by
the character of the people among whom he finds himself."[5]

As a critic of Virginians' "character," Jefferson was following a tradition
of other chroniclers of Virginia's history dating back to John Smith, who, in
writing about "the starving time" in 1609, refused to blame the environment

for the high death rate of the original settlers of Jamestown. "[T]he occasion was our owne," Smith wrote, "for want of providence, industrie and government, and not the barrenness and defect of the Countrie, as is generally supposed." Robert Beverley, who wrote a 1705 history of the colony, compared Virginia to "the Land of Promise" in the Bible, which by his calculations lay near the same latitude. "*Judea* was full of Rivers, and Branches of Rivers; So is Virginia. . . . Had that fertility of Soil? So has *Virginia*, equal to any Land in the known World. . . . In fine, if any one impartially considers all the Advantages of this Country, as Nature made it; he must allow it to be as fine a Place, as any in the Universe."[6]

But here was the rub: Virginians had failed to live up to Nature's promise. In Beverley's words, "They spunge upon the Blessings of a warm Sun, and a fruitful Soil. . . . I should be asham'd to publish this slothful Indolence of my Countrymen, but that I hope it will rouse them out of their Lethargy, and excite them to make the most of all of those happy Advantages which Nature has given them; and if it does this, I am sure they will have the Goodness to forgive me." According to historian Jack Greene, Beverley's *History* "revolved around an elaborate exploration of this palpable and intractable puzzle"—how "a country rendered so fine by nature had turned out to be in so many ways a profound cultural disappointment."[7]

Jefferson extended Beverley's admonitions by introducing a criticism of slavery into *Notes on the State of Virginia* and others of his writings. In Query XVIII in *Notes*, Jefferson offered the opinion that climate supported the institution of slavery, "For in a warm climate, no man will labour for himself who can make another labour for him. This is so true, that of the proprietors of slaves a very small proportion indeed are ever seen to labour." In the following query, Jefferson completed this thought with the observation that a dependence on the labor of slaves "begets subservience and venality, suffocates the germ of virtue, and prepares fit tools for the design of ambition."[8]

When his countrymen rebuffed his warnings to change their behaviors, Jefferson's reformist tendencies cooled, and he accepted the status quo. His second term as president took a severe emotional toll on him, and in the closing month of his tenure, he did not hide his desires to return to Monticello. To one correspondent, he wrote, "Within a few days I retire to my family, my books and farms. . . . Never did a prisoner, released from his chains, feel such relief as I shall on shaking off the shackles of power." To another, "Within two or three days I retire from scenes of difficulty,

President Franklin D. Roosevelt laying the cornerstone at the Thomas Jefferson Memorial on November 15, 1939. During his presidency, Roosevelt dealt with issues similar to those confronting Jefferson and Lincoln—especially the role of political parties in running the nation, federalism, presidential powers, and the proper political economy for the country. Like Jefferson and Lincoln, Roosevelt left the work of the nation unfinished. *Harris & Ewing, photographer, "President Lays Cornerstone of New Jefferson Memorial." Harris & Ewing Collection, Library of Congress.*

anxiety, and of contending passions, to the Elysium of domestic affections, and the irresponsible direction of my own affairs." To a third, "I am held by the cords of love to my family & country.... [W]ithin a few days I shall now bury myself in the groves of Monticello, & become a mere spectator of passing events."[9]

As he promised, when he returned to Monticello, he immersed himself in the agricultural rhythms and gentry lifestyle of Virginia. When an acquaintance asked in 1816 for Jefferson's assistance in calling for a constitutional convention in order to equalize representation in the state legislature, Jefferson declined to become involved. "I have not been in the habit," he wrote, "of mysterious reserve on any subject, nor of buttoning up my opinions within my own doublet [vest]. On the contrary, while in public service especially, I thought the public entitled to frankness, and intimately to know whom they employed. But I am now retired: I resign myself, as a passenger, with confidence to those at present at the helm, and ask but for rest, peace and good will."[10]

II

For Abraham Lincoln, life began at twenty-three, when he first achieved elected office in Illinois as a "Captain of Volunteers" in the Black Hawk War. This election, he later wrote in an autobiographical sketch, exceeded "any [other] success in [my] life." He was unsuccessful in his first attempt to be elected to the Illinois legislature following his three-month service in the war but took satisfaction in the fact that he carried his own precinct by a vote of 277 to 7. "This was the only time," he crowed, that "[I] was ever beaten on a direct vote of the people."[11]

In standing for election to the Illinois legislature in 1832 from Sangamon County, Lincoln attempted to convince voters that he was devoted to representing their wishes. "[I]n accordance with an established custom, and the principles of true republicanism," he wrote, "it becomes my duty to make known to you—the people whom I propose to represent—my sentiments with regard to local affairs."[12] He used similar words in 1836 after having successfully won the seat in 1834. Writing to the editor of the local newspaper, Lincoln promised that if reelected, "I shall consider the whole people of Sangamon my constituents, as well those that oppose, as those that support me. While acting as their representative, I shall be governed by their will, on all subjects upon which I have the means of knowing what their will is; and upon all others, I shall do what my own judgment teaches me will best advance their interests."[13]

Perhaps the most pressing question directly affecting his constituents concerned the location of the state capital: should it remain in Vandalia, where it was originally situated, or be moved to Springfield? Opponents of the move tried to weaken the influence of Sangamon County in the legislature by lopping off part of the county to form new counties, but Lincoln was instrumental in blocking this attempt. They also tried to derail the move by objecting to the cost of moving the capital and insinuating that private individuals stood to profit from such a move by buying up land adjacent to the capital. In a January 1839 speech, Lincoln admitted that he had relocated to Springfield in 1837 but denied that people were personally profiting from land speculation in the city.[14]

Lincoln's move from New Salem to Springfield allowed the young politician to hone his public-speaking skills at the Young Men's Lyceum and in numerous courtrooms across southern Illinois. Travel to other counties also allowed Lincoln to widen his renown and paved the way for his election to the US Congress in 1846. Service there thrust him directly into Whig opposition to the Mexican War but also revealed to Lincoln his unpreparedness to take a prominent role on the national stage. He admitted in October 1846 to his best friend from his early days in Springfield, Joshua Speed, that election to Congress "has not pleased me as much as I expected," and in January 1848, he wrote to his law partner, William Herndon, that he was uncomfortable speaking on the House floor. As a "way of getting the hang of the House," Lincoln reported, "I made a little speech . . . on a post-office question of no general interest. . . . I expect to make [another speech] within a week or two, in which I hope to succeed well enough to wish you to see it."[15] Although Whigs who were elected to Congress from Illinois pledged to serve only one term, Lincoln nonetheless tried to leave the door open to renomination. Writing to a constituent in April 1848, Lincoln said that he would stand behind his pledge not to seek reelection but that he "would deny the people nothing." He closed by cautioning, "Lest I be misunderstood, dont let any one know I have written you any thing on this subject."[16]

From the spring of 1849 until the fall of 1854, Lincoln did not seek public office. Lincoln scholars point to his October 16, 1854, address at Peoria, Illinois, against the Kansas-Nebraska Act as rekindling his political ambitions and offering him the possibility of extending them beyond the Springfield area.[17] For example, in his "House Divided" speech in June 1858, Lincoln warned the people of Illinois that the Supreme Court's Dred Scott decision was simply the starting point for making slavery legal everywhere in the nation (see chapter 1). Whatever Dred Scott's master "might lawfully do . . . ," Lincoln argued, "in the free state of Illinois, every other master may lawfully do with any other *one*, or one *thousand* slaves, in Illinois or any other free State." Were the Dred Scott decision to stand, Lincoln warned, the power of a state to decide the issue of slavery within its boundaries would be annulled. "We shall *lie down* pleasantly dreaming that the people of *Missouri* are on the verge of making their state *free*; and we shall *awake* to the *reality*, instead, that the *Supreme* Court has made *Illinois* a *slave* state."[18]

In the seven celebrated debates that Lincoln entered into with Stephen Douglas in the late summer and fall of 1858, his opponent portrayed Lincoln as a "Black Republican" and an abolitionist, references that Douglas believed would sink Republican hopes of gaining a majority in the Illinois legislature. For his part, Lincoln denied that he was present when either the national Republican Party platform of 1856 or the Illinois party platform of that year was constructed.[19] Further, Lincoln repeatedly avowed that he was not an abolitionist and argued that he did not support giving political or social equality to African Americans living in Illinois.

In addition, Douglas accused Lincoln of saying different things in northern and southern Illinois. For his part, Lincoln affirmed that he stood for the absolute right of the people of Illinois to determine the issues of slavery and African American rights in the state and denied that he tailored the content of his speeches to appeal to audiences in different sections of the state. For example, in the fourth debate, Lincoln responded to Douglas's charge by asking "every fair-minded man to take these speeches and read them, *and I dare him to point out any differences between my printed speeches north and south.*"[20] While it is true, as Douglas Wilson and others have observed, that Lincoln frequently altered his speeches before they were printed, Lincoln also countered that Douglas quoted selectively from the speeches in order to support his charge that Lincoln tailored the content of his speeches based on sectional differences. For example, in the seventh and final debate, Lincoln accused Douglas of "taking portions of a speech which, when taken by themselves, do not present the entire sense of the speaker as expressed at the time" and of skipping over other portions that "give a different idea and the true idea of what I intended to convey."[21]

Lincoln scholars agree that one should not conclude based on the fact that Illinois voters gave Democrats control of the state legislature that Lincoln failed to represent their wishes. What can be concluded is that Lincoln succeeded in attracting the attention of Republican leaders in Northern states, and following the election, Lincoln increased his attachment to the Republican Party. In a speech in March 1859 to Republican Party faithful at Chicago, Lincoln addressed the claim that Republicans would have been better suited to have endorsed Douglas for the Senate instead of Lincoln: "Let the Republican party of Illinois dally with Judge Douglas; let them fall in behind him and make him their candidate, and they do not absorb him; he absorbs them." In closing, Lincoln encouraged the members of the audience to stand behind the national and state Republican Party platforms: "All you have to do is keep the faith, to remain steadfast to the right, to stand by your banner. Nothing should lead you to leave your guns. Stand together, ready, with match in hand. . . . Stand by your principles; stand by your guns; and victory complete and permanent is sure at the last."[22]

He repeated the same message in private correspondence. For example, writing to a German American in May 1859, Lincoln said he was for "fusion" among groups "if it can be had on republican grounds." But, he said, "I am not for it on any other terms. . . . I am against letting down the republican standard a hair's breadth."[23] To Indiana senator Schuyler Colfax, Lincoln wrote in July 1859 that Republicans should endeavor in local conventions "to avoid everything which will distract republicans elsewhere. . . . In a word, in every locality we should look beyond our noses; and at least say *nothing* on points where it is probable we shall disagree."[24]

To promote his growing prominence within the Republican Party, Lincoln spoke in Ohio, Indiana, and Kansas in the fall of 1859 against Stephen A. Douglas in particular and the Democratic Party generally. The pinnacle of his growing prominence in the party occurred in February 1860, when he spoke at Cooper Institute in New York City. Speaking directly to members of his Republican Party at the close of his speech, he advised them that it was "*exceedingly desirable that all parts of this great Confederacy shall be at peace, and in harmony, with one another,*" but he also said that it would be hypocritical to yield to Southern demands if it meant giving up Republican Party principles. "Let us be diverted by none of those sophistical contrivances wherewith we are so industriously plied and belabored—contrivances such as groping for some middle ground between the right and the wrong. . . . LET US HAVE FAITH THAT RIGHT MAKES MIGHT, AND IN THAT FAITH, LET US, TO THE END, DARE TO DO OUR DUTY AS WE UNDERSTAND IT."[25]

As Lincoln transitioned from a person seeking office in Illinois to a leader in the Republican Party, he increasingly came to view himself as a Northerner. Writing to a leader in the Kansas Republican Party in May 1859, Lincoln said that he was not opposed to having Republicans try to bring Southerners into the party, but only if doing so did not mean emphasizing "questions which the people just now are really caring nothing about" and "ignoring the Slavery question." "I would cheerfully vote [for a Southerner] to be either President or Vice President," he averred, "provided he would enable me to do so with *safety* to the Republican cause—without lowering the Republican Standard. This is the indispensable condition of a union with us. It is idle to think of any other . . . , and it will result in gaining no single electoral vote in the *South* and losing ev[e]ry one in the North."[26] By the time of his Cooper Institute address, he knew that it was useless to maintain a fiction that the name of a Republican candidate for president in 1860 would appear on Southern ballots; therefore, he said that he would like to speak to Southerners about the issues of the day, "if I thought they would listen—as I suppose they will not."[27]

Immediately following his election as president, Lincoln's language was initially conciliatory. For example, in remarks at Springfield and Blooming-ton, Illinois, in November 1860, Lincoln advised supporters not to disparage "any citizen who, by his vote, has differed with us" and promised to "try to do well by [people] in all parts of the country, North and South, with entire confidence that all will be well with all of us."[28] As conventions in Southern states voted to secede, however, Lincoln repeated his statements that only Northerners wanted to save the nation in speeches on his way to Washington, DC, to be sworn in as president. For example, at Lafayette, Indiana, in February 1861, he told listeners, "I find myself far from home surrounded by the thousands I now see before me, who are strangers to me. Still we are bound together, I trust in christianity, civilization and patriotism, and are attached to our country and our whole country. . . . We all believe in the maintainance of the Union, of every star and every stripe of the glorious flag, and permit me to express the sentiment that upon the union of the States, there shall be between us no difference."[29]

In his first inaugural address, Lincoln tried to assuage Southerners' fears that he would invade their states in order to abolish slavery, but he aimed his message squarely at the Northern voters who had elected him president:

> Unanimity is impossible, the rule of a minority, as a permanent arrange-
> ment, is wholly inadmissible; so that, rejecting the majority principle, an-
> archy, or despotism in some form is all that is left. . . . Why should there
> not be a patient confidence in the ultimate justice of the people? Is there
> any better, or equal hope, in the world? In our present differences, is either
> party without faith of being in the right? If the Almighty Ruler of nations,
> with his eternal truth and justice, be on your side of the North, or on yours
> of the South, that truth and that justice, will surely prevail, by the judgment
> of this great tribunal, the American people.

He concluded the address by laying the issue of civil war squarely on secessionist Southerners: "In *your* hands, my dissatisfied fellow countrymen,
and not in *mine*, is the momentous issue of civil war. . . . You can have no
conflict, without being yourselves the aggressors."[30]

Toward the end of the war, however, as Lincoln confronted the reality
that the nation that ended the war had to be different from the one that
entered it, his perspective changed. As some members of his party sought
to punish Southerners for the war and opposed the presidential plan for
Reconstruction, Lincoln understood that following the war, Republicans
and Democrats, Northerners and Southerners, unionists and secessionists
somehow had to unite. In his response to a serenade following word of his
reelection as president in November 1864, Lincoln addressed not Republican or Northern voters, but all Americans: "[T]he rebellion continues;
and now that the election is over, may not all, having a common interest,
re-unite in a common effort, to save our common country? . . . While I am
deeply sensitive to the high compliment of a re-election; . . . it adds nothing
to my satisfaction that any other man may be disappointed or pained by
the result. May I ask those who have not differed with me, to join with me,
in this same spirit toward those who have?"[31] He continued this conciliatory spirit in his second inaugural address in March 1865, saying that the
war had begun because the American people were divided: "one . . . and
the other"; "[n]either party"; "[e]ach."[32] As Garry Wills has so convincingly
argued, Lincoln came to believe that only when *one people* offered a *common
prayer* could the nation hope to be reunited.[33]

III

In conclusion, both Jefferson and Lincoln drew strength from attachment
to place, which led each one to a devotion to promoting change. Jefferson
seldom missed an opportunity to tout his "country's" virtues, but he also
found reason to criticize the behavior of his fellow Virginians for not living
up to the possibilities that nature afforded them in such abundance. He
worried especially that a dependence on the labor of slaves was draining the
productive energies of the people. It is to Jefferson's credit that he saw so
clearly what his countrymen needed to do to escape from the past, but when
they resisted the changes that he advised, he did not follow through with
what he knew needed to be done. In the end, therefore, he accommodated

to the way things were and contented himself with the personal satisfaction that he had done all he could for Virginia.³⁴

Like Jefferson, Lincoln also saw things about his nation—the United States—that needed changing, such as slavery, addressed during his administration with the Emancipation Proclamation and the Thirteenth Amendment. Because he drew on his connections with people to locate himself in time and place, he moved beyond local attachments and came to adopt an Illinoisan, partisan, regional, and eventually national perspective. In doing so, Lincoln was able to redefine himself. By the time he gave his second inaugural address, he was drawing on the strength that he felt from the American people as he pledged to "bind up the nation's wounds."³⁵

Although Lincoln's attachment to different groups accorded him more latitude to reframe his positions on many issues, his dedication to promoting fundamental change in his society had limits. For example, it is questionable whether he would have been able to build a bridge between Northerners and Southerners following the war, and he may have felt the need to further modify his views of state rights. In addition, his devotion to extending voting rights to African Americans reached only veterans and "very intelligent" black people (see chapter 1), and he—as well as Jefferson—was unwilling to extend the same rights to women despite their sacrifices to the nation during the American Revolution and the Civil War. Because both Jefferson and Lincoln fell short of what they might have accomplished, they left to future generations the job of carrying forward their unfinished work.³⁶

———————————{ Postscript }———————————

I hope that this investigation of some of the ideas of these two prominent early American leaders will be a beginning point for further comparisons. I have not addressed issues where a preponderance of available evidence favors Jefferson over Lincoln, such as Native American relations or political and diplomatic entanglements with Great Britain. Neither have I addressed in depth the fact that both subscribed to a belief in majority rule, tempered by a respect for minority rights. Additionally, there are separate monographs for each devoted to a number of topics that might provide the basis for fruitful comparisons, including dealings with the Supreme Court, views of the West, and their relationships as presidents with the members of their cabinets.[1]

Areas of overlap between their life experiences also might generate fruitful inquiries using methodological perspectives that rely less on the two men's texts. For example, neither man was very close to his parents. Jefferson wrote approvingly of his father, Peter's, life as a frontier surveyor and planter in the Piedmont region of Virginia (the area between the coast and the Blue Ridge Mountains), but the exact influence of father on son remains obscure because Peter died in 1757, when Jefferson was only fourteen. Lincoln's father, Thomas, was a frontier farmer in Kentucky, Indiana, and Illinois, and son Abraham freed himself from his father's control as a lad of twenty-two. Once he left home, Lincoln never looked back; when Thomas died in 1851, Lincoln did not attend the funeral. Jefferson lived with his mother, Jane Randolph Jefferson (d. 1776), after his father's death, but according to most accounts, he was not close to her. Nancy Hanks Lincoln died in 1818, when her son Abraham was nine years old; he was much closer to his stepmother,

137

Sarah Johnston Lincoln (d. 1869), whom he credited with taking an interest in his intellectual development.

Both men also had difficult marriages and family lives. Jefferson married a widow, Martha Wayles Skelton, at the age of twenty-nine; she died as a result of complications attendant to the birth of their last child in 1782, after ten years of marriage. Following Martha's death, Jefferson never remarried, but he did develop a relationship with a married woman, the artist Maria Cosway, while he was minister to Paris, and he likely fathered the children of Sally Hemings, an enslaved woman at Monticello who was probably Martha's half sister. No letters from Jefferson to Martha exist, and most of his biographers accept the likelihood that he destroyed them. Lincoln married Mary Todd when he was thirty-three; she survived her husband, who died at age fifty-six. Both Lincolns were strong-willed individuals, and the presidential years took its toll on their relationship, especially following the death of son Willie in February 1862. Martha bore six children; Mary, four. Only one each of Martha's and Mary's children lived past the age of eighteen: Martha Jefferson Randolph lived into her sixties, and Robert Todd Lincoln lived to the age of eighty-three.

Health issues also were a burden for both men, especially difficulties each had from coping with stress. Jefferson suffered from migraine headaches that incapacitated him for days. In his later years, he had severe prostate problems. Lincoln also battled headaches and what was referred to in his time as "melancholy." His physical health was almost certainly in decline at the time of his death.

In addition to their remarkably fertile minds for political theory, both were inventors. Jefferson personally designed his homes and filled them with numerous inventions, including a dumbwaiter system for bringing Monticello's wine from the cellar to the dining room, the first parquet floor in an American home, and skylights at both Monticello and Poplar Forest. For his plantations, Jefferson perfected a plow—first made of wood and then of iron—that turned the earth more efficiently than other designs, but he never sought a patent on it. In fact, in an 1800 memorandum about his contributions to Virginia, he wrote, "The greatest service which can be rendered any country is, to add an useful plant to its culture"; the same may be said of his inventions.[2] For his part, Lincoln devised a system of assisting barges over shoals or other obstacles in a river by filling below-deck chambers with water that moved from one end of the boat to the other to improve buoyancy. Although there is no evidence that anyone ever marketed Lincoln's invention, he has the distinction of being the only man who owned a patent when he became president.[3]

Both began their political careers at an early age. Jefferson was elected to the Virginia House of Burgesses at age twenty-six; Lincoln won his first election to the Illinois legislature at twenty-five. Jefferson was elected president at fifty-eight; Lincoln, fifty-one. Both also viewed their elections as president as breaks with the past. Jefferson became estranged from President John Adams while serving as his vice president, especially because of Adams's (reluctant) support for the Alien and Sedition Acts and his desire to build a navy to protect American shipping. Lincoln criticized President James Buchanan's support for the Supreme Court's Dred Scott decision and the Democratic Party's failure to develop effective policies to save the nation from division in 1857–60.

Although the law was a common feature in their lives, they seem to have had more differences than similarities in their approaches to the profession. Whereas Jefferson apprenticed in Williamsburg with one of the nation's most prestigious attorneys, George Wythe, Lincoln was self-taught. Jefferson became a lawyer because most members of the Virginia gentry practiced law in addition to planting tobacco; Lincoln became a lawyer in order to improve himself. Jefferson did not like practicing law and actively engaged in it for only a few years; Lincoln made it his profession. Jefferson never enjoyed public speaking; Lincoln honed his speaking prowess—especially his ability to connect with his audience—before juries.

Debt was also a problem for both men, but overall they appear to have had more differences than similarities in the way they handled financial difficulties. Although Jefferson railed against banks specifically and commercial dealings in general, he, like most members of the Virginia gentry, lived continually in debt, and he died insolvent. Lincoln experienced financial difficulties early in his life, especially in connection with a store that he and a business associate established in New Salem, Illinois. The business failed, his partner died, and Lincoln was forced to declare bankruptcy. In contrast to Jefferson, however, Lincoln insisted on paying off both his and his partner's debts and later became financially secure because of his successful law practice.

Finally, the comparative approach employed in this work may also suggest to someone to carry the theme of "the unfinished work of the nation" forward to modern presidents. Topics like federalism, political parties, presidential powers under the Constitution, and political economy were also crucial to the administrations of Theodore Roosevelt, Woodrow Wilson, Franklin Roosevelt, and Ronald Reagan, to name only four. I will not speculate on whether such comparisons would be productive, but it would be interesting to see where they led. They might also generate productive civic discussions about why it has been so difficult for the nation to reach closure on these ideas.

ACKNOWLEDGMENTS

1. Ronald L. Hatzenbuehler, *"I Tremble for My Country": Thomas Jefferson and the Virginia Gentry* (Gainesville: University Press of Florida, 2006; paperback edition, 2009).
2. Michael P. Johnson, ed., *Abraham Lincoln, Slavery, and the Civil War: Selected Writings and Speeches* (Boston: Bedford/St. Martins, 2001).
3. Richard Hofstadter, *The American Political Tradition and the Men Who Made It* (New York: Alfred A. Knopf, 1948); Sean Wilentz, *The Rise of American Democracy: Jefferson to Lincoln* (New York: W. W. Norton & Company, 2005); Everett Eugene Edwards, *Washington, Jefferson, Lincoln and Agriculture* (Washington, DC: Bureau of Agricultural Economics, 1937).
4. See Merrill D. Peterson, *The Jefferson Image in the American Mind* (New York: Oxford University Press, 1960); *Lincoln in American Memory* (New York: Oxford University Press, 1994); *Adams and Jefferson: A Revolutionary Dialogue* (Athens: University of Georgia Press, 1976); and *The Great Triumvirate: Webster, Clay, and Calhoun* (New York: Oxford University Press, 1987).
5. F. Lauriston Bullard, "Lincoln as a Jeffersonian" (n.p., [1948?]). Allen Guelzo argues at length in the first chapter of *Abraham Lincoln: Redeemer President* (Grand Rapids, MI: William B. Eerdmans Publishing Co., 1999) that Lincoln and Jefferson as politicians were polar opposites, especially regarding their views of the proper political economy for the nation. He writes, for example, that "Abraham Lincoln grew and matured as an American political thinker into an adversary of almost every practical aspect of Thomas Jefferson's political worldview" (5). As will become apparent throughout this book (especially in chapter 6, devoted to political economy), I find both similarities and differences in the two men's views.
6. A case can be made, if one reads only their public statements, that both Jefferson and Lincoln subscribed to the idea of American exceptionalism. In private, however, they expressed doubts about whether the nation enjoyed a special status, especially if it is supposed that the nation's exceptionalism is rooted in a favored relationship with God (see chapter 4).
7. See, for example, *Idaho Humanities* 16, no. 1 (Winter 2012), http://www.idaho humanities.org/images/newsletters/2012wintervolxvino1.pdf. The views expressed in this book are my own and do not necessarily reflect those of either the Idaho Humanities Council or the National Endowment for the Humanities.

INTRODUCTION

1. Data from Statista: The Statistics Portal (accessed May 16, 2015): "Number of recreational visitors to the Lincoln Memorial in the United States from 2008 to 2014 (in millions)," http://www.statista.com/statistics/254029/number-of-visitors -to-the-lincoln-memorial/; "Number of recreational visitors to the Thomas Jefferson Memorial in the United States from 2008 to 2014 (in millions)," http://www .statista.com/statistics/254222/number-of-visitors-to-thomas-jefferson-memorial -in-the-us/; and "Number of recreational visitors to the Mount Rushmore National Memorial in the United States from 2008 to 2014 (in millions)," http://www.statista .com/statistics/254039/number-of-visitors-to-the-mount-rushmore-memorial/.

2. "Quotations on the Jefferson Memorial," Thomas Jefferson's Monticello, http:// www.monticello.org/site/jefferson/quotations-jefferson-memorial#Inscription _under_the_Dome (accessed May 30, 2015); "April 9, 1939: Marian Anderson Sings at Lincoln Memorial," History.com, http://www.history.com/this-day-in-history /marian-anderson-sings-at-lincoln-memorial (accessed May 30, 2015); "We Shall Overcome: Lincoln Memorial," National Park Service, http://www.nps.gov/nr /travel/civilrights/dc1.htm (accessed Nov. 9, 2015).

3. See, especially, Abraham Lincoln, "Speech in Independence Hall, Philadelphia, Pennsylvania," Feb. 22, 1861, in *The Collected Works of Abraham Lincoln*, ed. Roy P. Basler (New Brunswick, NJ: Rutgers University Press, 1953), 3:240. Historian Allen Guelzo argues—relying on remembrances of Lincoln's law partner William Herndon and a speech that Lincoln may have given in 1844 while campaigning for Henry Clay's presidential bid that year—that Lincoln believed Jefferson was a hypocrite whose actions did not correspond with his words; see Guelzo, *Abraham Lincoln*, 3–4. Guelzo attributes Lincoln's about-face regarding his views on Jefferson to the fact that the Virginian had become an American icon by the 1850s and that it was politically shrewd for Lincoln to emphasize that the Democratic Party had embraced a single-minded commitment to protecting slaveholding in the South. I do not deny Lincoln's political shrewdness but emphasize an alternative perspective that after 1854, he saw that *Jefferson's words* could provide the moral underpinning for instituting fundamental changes in the American political system.

4. Lincoln to Henry L. Pierce and Others, Apr. 6, 1859, *Collected Works*, 3:375.

5. Lincoln, "Message to Congress in Special Session," July 4, 1861, *Collected Works*, 4:421–41; Lincoln, "Address Delivered at the Dedication of the Cemetery at Gettysburg," Nov. 19, 1863, *Collected Works*, 7:23.

6. Lincoln, "Address Delivered at the Dedication of the Cemetery at Gettysburg," Nov. 19, 1863, *Collected Works*, 7:23 (emphasis added).

7. Lincoln, "Second Inaugural Address," Mar. 4, 1865, *Collected Works*, 8:333 (emphasis added).

8. Thomas Jefferson to Roger C. Weightman, June 24, 1826, in *The Portable Thomas Jefferson*, ed. Merrill D. Peterson (New York: Viking Penguin Books, 1975), 585.

9. Quoted in William H. Herndon and Jesse W. Weik, *Herndon's Lincoln*, ed. Douglas L. Wilson and Rodney O. Davis (Urbana: University of Illinois Press, 2006), 312. Historian Richard Current emphasizes that by all accounts, Lincoln was a slow thinker who returned throughout his life to key themes and in the process "steadily improved his phrasing." Current, *The Lincoln Nobody Knows* (New York: McGraw-Hill, 1958), 9.

10. Jefferson, *Notes on the State of Virginia, Portable Jefferson*, 215.

11. Lincoln, "Response to a Serenade," Feb. 1, 1865, *Collected Works*, 8:254.

12. Whereas the Articles of Confederation acknowledged that states were sovereign entities (i.e., acting as countries), the Constitution established a federal system of government by dividing or sharing government's powers between the nation and the states. Antifederalists, however, made a telling argument that the people and the states had *reserved rights* that were not enumerated in the Constitution, and James Madison saw the wisdom of clarifying that point with the Bill of Rights, which expressly stated some rights (Amendments I–VIII) but left others vague (Amendments IX and X). The nation is still working out the meaning of the Ninth Amendment, but discussion regarding the Tenth Amendment began quickly, stimulated by Alexander Hamilton's rationale for the First National Bank, that Congress had the power to create such an institution under the "necessary and proper" clause of Article I, Section 8. Jefferson and Madison disputed Hamilton's claims by arguing that Congress could not of itself decide what was "necessary and proper," and Jefferson wrote in his Kentucky Resolutions that the states *acting collectively* ("states' rights") should check the powers of the national government when it acted outside of its expressed powers. Then in the 1830s, the state of South Carolina twisted Jefferson's understanding of "states' rights" when it *acted alone* to nullify a tariff bill, and John C. Calhoun extended that argument to include the right of a state to secede from the United States. Lincoln in his July 4, 1861, address to Congress coined the term "state rights" to refer to the rights that a state enjoyed under federalism and to negate the view that each state had the ability to act as a sovereign entity.

13. Jefferson to Major John Cartwright, June 5, 1824, *Portable Jefferson*, 581.

14. Lincoln, "Address to the New Jersey Senate at Trenton, New Jersey," Feb. 21, 1861, *Collected Works*, 4:236.

15. Jefferson, "A Bill for Establishing Religious Freedom," [1777], *Portable Jefferson*, 251–52.

16. Jefferson to Nehemiah Dodge and Others, a Committee of the Danbury Baptist Association, in the State of Connecticut, Jan. 1, 1802, *Portable Jefferson*, 303–4.

17. Jefferson to John Breckinridge, Aug. 12, 1803, *Portable Jefferson*, 497.

18. Jefferson, *Notes, Portable Jefferson*, 217; Jefferson, "First Inaugural Address," *Portable Jefferson*, 294; Jefferson to Benjamin Austin, Jan. 9, 1816, *Portable Jefferson*, 549.

19. Lincoln, "Communication to the People of Sangamo County," Mar. 9, 1832, *Collected Works*, 1:8.

20. Lincoln, "Address before the Wisconsin State Agricultural Society, Milwaukee, Wisconsin," Sept. 30, 1859, *Collected Works*, 3:471–82.
21. This sentence owes its wording to a statement by George Will that George Washington *fought* for the nation in the American Revolution and that Thomas Jefferson *thought* for it. Thomas Jefferson Foundation, *Thomas Jefferson: The Pursuit of Liberty* (New York: Films for the Humanities & Sciences, 1991), video recording.

1. "IN *GIVING* FREEDOM TO THE *SLAVE,* WE *ASSURE* FREEDOM TO THE *FREE*"

1. Larry L. King, *Confessions of a White Racist* (New York: Viking Press, 1971), 16–17.
2. T. H. Breen, "Looking Out for Number One," *South Atlantic Quarterly* 78 (Summer 1979): 342–60.
3. Jefferson, *A Summary View of the Rights of British America*, [1774], *Portable Jefferson*, 14–15.
4. Jefferson, "Declaration of Independence," [July 1776], *Portable Jefferson*, 238–39.
5. Jefferson, "Draft Constitution for Virginia," [June 1776], *Portable Jefferson*, 337, 344; "Report on Government for Western Territory," Mar. 1, 1784, in *Thomas Jefferson: Writings*, ed. Merrill D. Peterson (New York: Library of America, 1984), 377.
6. Jefferson, *Notes*, *Portable Jefferson*, 186, 193. The presence of the mulatto members of the Hemings family at Monticello, however, and the likelihood that Jefferson fathered Sally Hemings's children indicate that he ignored this advice for himself; see Douglas Egerton, "Thomas Jefferson and the Hemings Family: A Matter of Blood," *Historian* 59 (1997): 327–45. Archaeologist Susan Kern suggests that Sandy and Sawney—slaves of Jefferson's father, Peter—were the sons of Peter and his father, respectively; see *The Jeffersons at Shadwell* (New Haven, CT: Yale University Press, 2010), 112.
7. Jefferson, *Notes*, *Portable Jefferson*, 215.
8. Thomas Jefferson to James Madison, May 11, 1785, in *Papers of Thomas Jefferson*, ed. Julian Boyd (Princeton, NJ: Princeton University Press, 1950), 8:148.
9. Jefferson to Chastellux, June 7, 1785, *Papers*, 8:184.
10. Douglas R. Egerton, *Gabriel's Rebellion: The Virginia Slave Conspiracies of 1800 & 1802* (Chapel Hill: University of North Carolina Press, 1993), 154, 160–61, 168–72.
11. Jefferson to Edward Coles, Aug. 25, 1814, *Portable Jefferson*, 544–45.
12. Ibid., 546.
13. Ibid., 547.
14. Elizabeth Langhorne, "Edward Coles, Thomas Jefferson, and the Rights of Man," *Virginia Cavalcade* 23 (1973–74): 30–37; Suzanne Cooper Guasco, *Confronting Slavery: Edward Coles and the Rise of Antislavery Politics in Nineteenth-Century America* (DeKalb: Northern Illinois University Press, 2013).
15. Jefferson to Samuel Kercheval, July 12, 1816, *Portable Jefferson*, 552–53. See also Jefferson to Jared Sparks, Feb. 4, 1824, Peterson, *Writings*, 1484.

16. Because most houses in early America were made of wood, the ringing of a "fire-bell" meant that all residents should turn out with buckets to squelch the flames. Jefferson to John Holmes, Apr. 22, 1820, *Portable Jefferson*, 568. See also Jefferson to Albert Gallatin, Dec. 26, 1820, Peterson, *Writings*, 1450.

17. Ellen Randolph Coolidge to Thomas Jefferson, Aug. 1, 1825; Thomas Jefferson to Ellen Randolph Coolidge, Aug. 25, 1825, in *Family Letters of Thomas Jefferson*, ed. Edwin Morris Betts and James Adam Bear Jr. (Columbia: University of Missouri Press, 1966), 454–58.

18. Lincoln to Williamson Durley, Oct. 3, 1845, *Collected Works*, 1:347.

19. Lincoln, "Speech at Worcester, Massachusetts," Sept. 12, 1848, *Collected Works*, 2:3.

20. Lincoln, "Eulogy on Henry Clay," July 6, 1852, *Collected Works*, 2:130.

21. Ibid., 2:132.

22. Lincoln, "Speech at Peoria, Illinois," Oct. 16, 1854, *Collected Works*, 2:275.

23. Ibid., 2:268.

24. Lincoln, "Seventh and Last Debate with Stephen A. Douglas at Alton, Illinois," Oct. 15, 1858, *Collected Works*, 3:312.

25. Lincoln, "Speech at Peoria, Illinois," Oct. 16, 1854, *Collected Works*, 2:269–70.

26. Ibid., 2:266.

27. Lincoln to George Robertson, Aug. 15, 1855, *Collected Works*, 2:318; Lincoln to Joshua F. Speed, Aug. 24, 1855, *Collected Works*, 2:322.

28. Lincoln, "'A House Divided': Speech at Springfield, Illinois," June 16, 1858, *Collected Works*, 2:461, 467.

29. Lincoln, "Address at Cooper Institute," Feb. 27, 1860, *Collected Works*, 3:548; "Speech at Hartford, Connecticut," Mar. 5, 1860, *Collected Works*, 4:8.

30. Stephen A. Douglas in Lincoln, "First Debate with Stephen A. Douglas at Ottawa, Illinois," Aug. 21, 1858, *Collected Works*, 3:9.

31. Lincoln, "Seventh and Last Debate with Stephen A. Douglas at Alton, Illinois," Oct. 15, 1858, *Collected Works*, 3:315.

32. Lincoln, "First Debate with Stephen A. Douglas at Ottawa, Illinois," Aug. 21, 1858, *Collected Works*, 3:16; "Seventh and Last Debate with Stephen A. Douglas at Alton, Illinois," Oct. 15, 1858, *Collected Works*, 3:301.

33. Lincoln, "Annual Message to Congress," Dec. 3, 1861, *Collected Works*, 5:48.

34. Lincoln, "Address on Colonization to a Deputation of Negroes," Aug. 14, 1862, *Collected Works*, 5:371–72.

35. Lincoln to Horace Greeley, Aug. 22, 1862, *Collected Works*, 5:388–89.

36. Lincoln, "Reply to Emancipation Memorial Presented by Chicago Christians of All Denominations," Sept. 13, 1862, *Collected Works*, 5:423.

37. Historian David Donald writes that Congress's passage on July 17, 1862, of the Second Confiscation Act and the Militia Act of 1862, which declared slaves of rebels to be free and authorized the president to use them for military service, pressured Lincoln into issuing the Emancipation Proclamation; see Donald, *Lincoln* (New York: Simon & Schuster, 1995), 366–67.

38. Lincoln, "Preliminary Emancipation Proclamation," Sept. 22, 1862, *Collected Works*, 5:433–36; "Emancipation Proclamation," Jan. 1, 1863, *Collected Works*, 6: 28–30; "Reply to Emancipation Memorial Presented by Chicago Christians of All Denominations," Sept. 13, 1862, *Collected Works*, 5:423; "Annual Message to Congress," Dec. 1, 1862, *Collected Works*, 5:534, 537.

39. Eric Foner, *The Fiery Trial: Abraham Lincoln and American Slavery* (New York: W. W. Norton, 2010), xx–xxi; see also John David Smith, *Lincoln and the U.S. Colored Troops* (Carbondale: Southern Illinois University Press, 2013).

40. Lincoln, "Order of Retaliation," July 30, 1863, *Collected Works*, 6:357.

41. Lincoln, "Annual Message to Congress," Dec. 8, 1863, *Collected Works*, 7:51.

42. Lincoln, "Speech in Independence Hall, Philadelphia, Pennsylvania," Feb. 22, 1861, *Collected Works*, 4:240.

43. Garry Wills, *Lincoln at Gettysburg: The Words That Remade America* (New York: Simon & Schuster, 1992).

44. Lincoln, "Address Delivered at the Dedication of the Cemetery at Gettysburg," Nov. 19, 1863 (Final Text), *Collected Works*, 7:23 (emphasis added).

45. Lincoln, "Reply to Committee Notifying Lincoln of His Renomination," June 9, 1864, *Collected Works*, 7:380 (brackets added by Basler).

46. Roy P. Basler, "Editorial Note," *Collected Works*, 8:254.

47. Lincoln, "Response to a Serenade," Feb. 1, 1865, *Collected Works*, 8:254–55.

48. Lincoln, "Last Public Address," Apr. 11, 1865, *Collected Works*, 8:403–4.

49. Jefferson, *Notes*, *Portable Jefferson*, 192–93.

50. David Williams, *I Freed Myself: African American Self-Emancipation in the Civil War Era* (New York: Cambridge University Press, 2014), 1.

2. "YOU ENQUIRE WHERE I NOW STAND"

1. See Richard Hofstadter, *The Idea of a Party System: The Rise of Legitimate Opposition in the United States, 1780–1840* (Berkeley: University of California Press, 1970).

2. Jefferson to Francis Hopkinson, Mar. 13, 1789, *Portable Jefferson*, 435–37.

3. Alexander Hamilton, James Madison, and John Jay, *The Federalist Papers*, ed. Clinton Rossiter (New York: New American Library, 1961), 112, 152.

4. Ibid., 246.

5. Ibid., 323, 83.

6. Jefferson to Philip Mazzei, Apr. 24, 1796, *Portable Jefferson*, 470–71.

7. Jefferson, "First Inaugural Address," Mar. 4, 1801, *Portable Jefferson*, 291–92; Jefferson to Spencer Roane, Sept. 6, 1819, *Portable Jefferson*, 562.

8. Jefferson also invited Federalist congressmen to separate dinners. See especially Noble E. Cunningham Jr., *The Process of Government under Jefferson* (Princeton, NJ: Princeton University Press, 1978).

9. Jefferson to John Melish, Jan. 13, 1813, Peterson, *Writings*, 1268.

10. Jefferson to Lafayette, May 14, 1817, Peterson, *Writings*, 1407–8. The Federalist Party's last candidate for the presidency was New York senator Rufus King in 1816.

11. Jefferson to John Holmes, Apr. 22, 1820, *Portable Jefferson*, 568; Jefferson to Albert Gallatin, Dec. 26, 1820, Peterson, *Writings*, 1448–49.

12. Jefferson to William Johnson, Oct. 27, 1822, Peterson, *Writings*, 1462–63. See also Jefferson to William Johnson, June 12, 1823, Peterson, *Writings*, 1472.

13. Lincoln became active in local Whig politics in the late 1830s. See Lincoln to John T. Stuart, Nov. 14, 1839, *Collected Works*, 1:154. For his growing attachment to the party, see Lincoln to Williamson Durley, Oct. 3, 1848, *Collected Works*, 1:347–48.

14. Lincoln to Thomas S. Flournoy, Feb. 17, 1848, *Collected Works*, 1:452; Lincoln to Usher F. Linder, Feb. 20, 1848, *Collected Works*, 1:453; Lincoln to Archibald Williams, Apr. 30, 1848, *Collected Works*, 1:468.

15. Lincoln to William H. Herndon, *Collected Works*, June 12, 1848, 1:477.

16. Lincoln, "Speech to the Springfield Scott Club," Aug. 14, 26, 1852, *Collected Works*, 2:135–57; "Speech at Peoria, Illinois," Sept. 17, 1852, *Collected Works*, 2:158–59.

17. Lincoln, "Eulogy on Henry Clay," July 6, 1852, *Collected Works*, 2:126.

18. Lincoln to Ichabod Cotting, Nov. 27, 1854, *Collected Works*, 2:288.

19. Ibid.

20. Lincoln to Owen Lovejoy, Aug. 11, 1854, *Collected Works*, 2:316–17.

21. Lincoln to Joshua F. Speed, Aug. 24, 1854, *Collected Works*, 2:322–23.

22. As examples, see Lincoln, "Speech at Galena, Illinois," July 23, 1856, *Collected Works*, 2:353–55; "Speech at Kalamazoo, Michigan," Aug. 27, 1856, *Collected Works*, 2:361–66; "Speech at Petersburg, Illinois," Aug. 30, 1856, *Collected Works*, 2:368–73; "Speech at Belleville, Illinois," Oct. 18, 1856; *Collected Works*, 2:379–80.

23. See Lincoln, "Form Letter to Fillmore Men," Sept. 8, 1856, *Collected Works*, 2:374; "Speech at a Republican Banquet," Dec. 10, 1856; *Collected Works*, 2:383–85.

24. Lincoln to John Bennett, Aug. 4, 1856, *Collected Works*, 2:358.

25. Lincoln, "Fragment on Formation of the Republican Party," Feb. 28, 1857, *Collected Works*, 2:391. See also Lincoln, "Speech at a Republican Banquet, Chicago, Illinois," Dec. 10, 1856, *Collected Works*, 2:383–85.

26. Lincoln, "Address at Cooper Institute, New York City," Feb. 27, 1860, *Collected Works*, 3:536. See also Lincoln, "Speech at Manchester, New Hampshire," Mar. 1, 1860, *Collected Works*, 3:551.

27. Lincoln to Truman Smith, Nov. 10, 1860, *Collected Works*, 4:138.

28. Lincoln, "Speech at the Astor House, New York City," Feb. 19, 1861, *Collected Works*, 4:230–31.

29. Lincoln, "First Inaugural Address," Mar. 4, 1861, *Collected Works*, 4:271.

30. Lincoln, "Address at Cooper Institute, New York City," Feb. 27, 1860, *Collected Works*, 3:537.

31. Lincoln, "Proclamation Revoking General Hunter's Order of Military Emancipation of May 9, 1862," *Collected Works*, 5:223.

32. Lincoln to Erastus Corning and Others, [June 12] 1863, *Collected Works*, 6:267–68.

33. Lincoln to Carl Schurz, Nov. 24, 1862, *Collected Works*, 5:509–10.

34. Lincoln to James C. Conkling, Aug. 26, 1863, *Collected Works*, 6:409.

35. Lincoln, "Proclamation of Amnesty and Reconstruction," Dec. 8, 1863, *Collected Works*, 7:53–56; "Annual Message to Congress," Dec. 8, 1863, *Collected Works*, 7:52.
36. Lincoln, "Proclamation Concerning Reconstruction," July 8, 1864, *Collected Works*, 7:433.
37. Lincoln to William T. Sherman, Sept. 19, 1864, *Collected Works*, 8:11.
38. Lincoln, "Speech to One Hundred Eighty-Ninth New York Volunteers," Oct. 24, 1864, *Collected Works*, 8:75.
39. Lincoln, "Response to a Serenade," Nov. 8, 1864, *Collected Works*, 8:96. Republicans changed the name of their party to the National Union Party in preparation for the election of 1864, but splinter groups persisted within it.
40. Lincoln, "Last Public Address," Apr. 11, 1865, *Collected Works*, 8:401–5.

3. "WHENCE THIS MAGICAL OMNIPOTENCE OF 'STATE RIGHTS' . . . ?"

1. Michael Shaara, *The Killer Angels* (New York: Ballantine Books, 1974), 170–71.
2. See Edmund S. Morgan, *Inventing the People: The Rise of Popular Sovereignty in England and America* (New York: W. W. Norton & Company, 1988).
3. During the bicentennial celebration of the drafting of the Constitution, a *Wall Street Journal*/NBC News poll asked a group of Americans to name the person who played the "biggest role" in drafting the Constitution. Not surprisingly, the majority answer was "Don't Know," but Jefferson was a close second, at 31 percent, and only 1 percent named James Madison. *Wall Street Journal*, Nov. 28, 1986, A1, A7.
4. Jefferson to John Adams, Nov. 13, 1787, Peterson, *Writings*, 913–14.
5. Jefferson to James Madison, Dec. 20, 1787, Peterson, *Writings*, 915–19.
6. Jefferson to Alexander Donald, Feb. 2, 1788, Peterson, *Writings*, 919–20; Jefferson to William Carmichael, June 3, 1788, *Papers*, 13:232–33; Jefferson to Thomas Lee Shippen, June 19, 1788, *Papers*, 13:277; Jefferson to John Brown Cutting, July 8, 1788, *Papers*, 13:315–16.
7. Jefferson, "Opinion on the Constitutionality of a National Bank," Feb. 15, 1791, *Portable Jefferson*, 267.
8. Jefferson to George Washington, Sept. 9, 1792, *Portable Jefferson*, 456, 459.
9. Jefferson, "Memoranda of Conversations with the President," Mar. 1, 1792, *Papers*, 23:284.
10. Jefferson, "The Anas," [1791–1806], Peterson, *Writings*, 671.
11. Ibid., 672.
12. Thomas Jefferson to James Madison, Oct. 26, 1798, in *The Republic of Letters*, ed. James Morton Smith (New York: Norton, 1995), 2:1077–78.
13. Jefferson, "The Kentucky Resolutions," [October 1798], *Portable Jefferson*, 281, 285–86.
14. Ibid., 285–86.
15. Ibid., 286, 289.
16. Ibid., 289.
17. Jefferson to John Taylor, June 1, 1798, Peterson, *Writings*, 475–76.

18. Jefferson to A. L. C. Destutt de Tracy, Jan. 26, 1811, *Portable Jefferson*, 523–25.
19. Jefferson to John Melish, Jan. 13, 1813, Peterson, *Writings*, 1269.
20. Jefferson to William Branch Giles, Dec. 26, 1825, Peterson, *Writings*, 1509–11.
21. Jefferson, "Autobiography," Jan. 6, 1821, Peterson, *Writings*, 70–71.
22. Jefferson, "First Inaugural Address," Mar. 4, 1801, *Portable Jefferson*, 293.
23. Lincoln, "Speech at Peoria, Illinois," Oct. 16, 1854, *Collected Works*, 2:247–83.
24. Lincoln, "'A House Divided': Speech at Springfield, Illinois," June 16, 1858, *Collected Works*, 2:461–62.
25. Lincoln, "Speech at Columbus, Ohio," Sept. 16, 1859, *Collected Works*, 3:419.
26. Ibid., 3:408–9.
27. Michael J. McManus, "'Freedom and Liberty First, and the Union Afterwards': State Rights and the Wisconsin Republican Party, 1854–1861," in *Union & Emancipation: Essays on Politics and Race in the Civil War Era*, ed. David Blight and Brooks Simpson (Kent, OH: Kent State University Press, 1997), 29–56, 189–97.
28. Lincoln, "Speech at Cooper Institute, New York City," Feb. 27, 1860, *Collected Works*, 3:532, 535.
29. Ibid., 3:535, 543.
30. Ibid., 3:544–46.
31. Ibid., 3:547, 550.
32. Lincoln to Alexander H. Stephens, Dec. 22, 1860, *Collected Works*, 4:160.
33. Lincoln to Duff Green, Dec. 28, 1860, *Collected Works*, 4:162–63.
34. Lincoln, "Speech from the Balcony of the Bates House at Indianapolis, Indiana," Feb. 11, 1861, *Collected Works*, 4:195–96.
35. Lincoln, "First Inaugural Address—First Edition and Revisions," Mar. 4, 1861, *Collected Works*, 4:250, 256, 260.
36. Lincoln, "Address to a Special Session of Congress," July 4, 1861, *Collected Works*, 4:433–34.
37. Ibid., 4:435.
38. Ibid., 4:434, 437–38.
39. Ibid., 4:439.
40. Lincoln to Beriah Magoffin, Aug. 24, 1861, *Collected Works*, 4:497.
41. Lincoln, "Opinion on the Admission of West Virginia into the Union," [Dec. 31, 1862], *Collected Works*, 6:27–28.
42. Lincoln, "First Inaugural Address," Mar. 4, 1861, *Collected Works*, 4:268. See also Lincoln, "Speech at Steubenville, Ohio," Feb. 14, 1861, *Collected Works*, 4:207.

4. "RELIGIOUS OPINIONS OR BELIEF"

1. Jefferson, "First Inaugural Address," Mar. 4, 1801, *Portable Jefferson*, 291; [Hartford] *Connecticut Courant*, November 2, 9, 1801.
2. *Boston Independent Chronicle & Universal Advertiser*, March 16–19, 1801.
3. Jefferson to Chastellux, June 7, 1785, Peterson, *Writings*, 799.
4. Jefferson, *Notes*, *Portable Jefferson*, 210.

5. Jefferson, "A Bill for Establishing Religious Freedom," [1777], *Portable Jefferson*, 251–53. The italics indicate the portions cut by the Virginia Assembly from the Statute for Religious Freedom that it eventually adopted in 1786.

6. Jefferson, *Notes*, *Portable Jefferson*, 48–49.

7. Ibid., 60–61.

8. Ibid., 63.

9. Jefferson to Nehemiah Dodge and Others, a Committee of the Danbury Baptist Association, in the State of Connecticut, Jan. 1, 1802, *Portable Jefferson*, 303–4.

10. "Religion and the Founding of the American Republic Religion and the Federal Government, Part 1," Library of Congress, http://www.loc.gov/exhibits/religion /rel06.html (accessed Mar. 3, 2015).

11. Jefferson, "First Inaugural Address," Mar. 4, 1801, *Portable Jefferson*, 295; Jefferson, "Second Inaugural Address," Mar. 4, 1805, Peterson, *Writings*, 523.

12. "Religion and the Founding of the American Republic Religion and the Federal Government, Part 2," Library of Congress, http://www.loc.gov/exhibits/religion /rel06-2.html (accessed Mar. 3, 2015).

13. Jefferson to Rev. Samuel Miller, Jan 23, 1808, Peterson, *Writings*, 1186–87.

14. Jefferson to Benjamin Rush, Apr. 21, 1803, *Portable Jefferson*, 490–94.

15. Jefferson to Mrs. Samuel H. Smith, Aug. 6, 1816, Peterson, *Writings*, 1404.

16. Jefferson to William Short, Oct. 31, 1819, *Portable Jefferson*, 565.

17. Lincoln, "Handbill Replying to Charges of Infidelity," July 31, 1846, *Collected Works*, 1:382.

18. Ibid. It is interesting to note that Jefferson used similar language in defending his belief "in the general existence of a moral instinct" and paraphrased language of Henry Home, Lord Kames, "in his Principles of Natural Religion, that a man owes no duty to which he is not urged by some impulsive feeling." Jefferson to Thomas Law, June 13, 1814, *Portable Jefferson*, 543.

19. Lincoln, "Address before the Young Men's Lyceum of Springfield, Illinois," Jan. 27, 1838, *Collected Works*, 1:115; "Speech at Chicago, Illinois," July 10, 1858, *Collected Works*, 2:501.

20. Lincoln, "Farewell Address at Springfield, Illinois," Feb. 11, 1861, *Collected Works*, 4:190; "Speech at Cincinnati, Ohio," Feb. 12, 1861, *Collected Works*, 4:199; "Address to the Ohio Legislature," Feb. 13, 1861, *Collected Works*, 4:204; "Address to the Legislature at Albany, New York," Feb. 18, 1861, *Collected Works*, 4:226; "First Inaugural Address," Mar. 4, 1861, *Collected Works*, 4:270.

21. Mark A. Noll, *The Civil War as a Theological Crisis* (Chapel Hill: University of North Carolina Press, 2006), 14, 27.

22. Lincoln, "Address to the New Jersey Senate at Trenton, New Jersey," Feb. 21, 1861, *Collected Works*, 4:236 (emphasis added).

23. Lincoln, "Meditation on Divine Will," [Sept. 2, 1862?], *Collected Works*, 5:403–4.

24. Basler, "Ed. Note," *Collected Works*, 4:404.

25. Ronald C. White Jr., *Lincoln's Greatest Speech: The Second Inaugural* (New York: Simon & Schuster Paperbacks, 2002), 122.

26. Basler, "Ed. Note.," *Collected Works*, 5:419; Lincoln, "Reply to Emancipation Memorial Presented by Chicago Christians of All Denominations," Sept. 13, 1862, *Collected Works*, 5:419–20.

27. In his biography of Lincoln, Ronald C. White Jr. revises his earlier dating of the document and states that Lincoln wrote the Meditation "[a]t some point during the latter part of his presidency." *A. Lincoln: A Biography* (New York: Random House, 2010), 622.

28. Lincoln, "Annual Message to Congress," Dec. 1, 1862, *Collected Works*, 5:518, 537.

29. Lincoln to James C. Conkling, Aug. 26, 1863, *Collected Works*, 6:410; "Address Delivered at the Dedication of the Cemetery at Gettysburg," Nov. 19, 1863, *Collected Works*, 7:23. Lincoln may have extemporaneously added the phrase "under God" to his draft remarks; alternatively, a newspaper reporter may have inserted it. What can be ascertained is that Lincoln included it in written copies that he made after his speech. See Wills, *Lincoln at Gettysburg*, 191–203.

30. Lincoln to Mrs. Horace Mann, Apr. 5, 1864, *Collected Works*, 7:287; "Address at Sanitary Fair," Apr. 18, 1864, *Collected Works*, 7:301.

31. Lincoln to Eliza P. Gurney, Sept. 4, 1864, *Collected Works*, 7:535; "Response to a Serenade," Nov. 10, 1864, *Collected Works*, 8:101. Based on the content of the letter to Gurney, Harry S. Stout dates the "Meditation on the Divine Will" to September 1864. Stout, "Lincoln's God and the Emancipation Proclamation," paper presented at Virginia Union University, May 2013. I am grateful to Professor Stout for sharing this unpublished paper with me.

32. Lincoln, "Second Inaugural Address," Mar. 4, 1865, *Collected Works*, 8:333; David Herbert Donald, *Lincoln* (New York: Simon & Schuster, 1995), 567.

33. Lincoln, "Second Inaugural Address," Mar. 4, 1865, *Collected Works*, 8:333; "Address to the New Jersey Senate at Trenton, New Jersey," Feb. 21, 1861, *Collected Works*, 4:236; "Meditation on Divine Will," [Sept. 2, 1862?], *Collected Works*, 5:403–4; Lincoln to Eliza P. Gurney, Sept. 4, 1864, *Collected Works*, 7:535.

34. Lincoln, "Second Inaugural Address," Mar. 4, 1865, *Collected Works*, 8:333 (emphasis added).

35. Ibid. (emphasis added).

36. In *A. Lincoln*, Ronald C. White Jr. expresses the view that Lincoln believed that God intervenes in human history, whereas Jefferson did not (624).

37. Lincoln to Thurlow Weed, Mar. 15, 1865, *Collected Works*, 8:356.

38. Jefferson, "To Nehemiah Dodge, and Others, a Committee of the Danbury Baptist Association, in the State of Connecticut," Jan. 1, 1802, *Portable Jefferson*, 303; Lincoln, "Meditation on Divine Will," [Sept. 2, 1862?], *Collected Works*, 5:403–4.

5. "ACT[S] OF INDEMNITY"

1. "About Oath Keepers," Oathkeepers.org, http://oathkeepers.org (accessed Feb. 26, 2015).

2. "Extremism in America: Council of Concerned Citizens," Anti-Defamation League, http://63.146.172.78/learn/ext_us/CCCitizens.asp?LEARN_Cat=Extremism &LEARN_SubCat=Extremism_in_America&xpicked=3&item=ccc (accessed Feb. 26, 2015).

3. Jefferson to John Breckinridge, Aug. 12, 1803, *Portable Jefferson*, 497. See also Thomas Jefferson, "Gentlemen of the Senate," Oct. 17, 1803, and "To the Senate and House of Representatives of the United States," Oct. 21, 1803, in *A Compilation of the Messages and Papers of the Presidents*, ed. James D. Richardson (Washington, DC: Bureau of National Literature and Art, 1897), 1:350–51.

4. Lincoln, "Message to Congress in Special Session," July 4, 1861, *Collected Works*, 4:433.

5. Jefferson, "Opinion on the Constitutionality of a National Bank," Feb. 15, 1791, *Portable Jefferson*, 262.

6. Jefferson to George Washington, Sept. 9, 1792, *Portable Jefferson*, 455–57.

7. Hamilton, Madison, and Jay, *Federalist Papers*, 36.

8. Jefferson to James Monroe, Sept. 7, 1798, *Papers*, 29:526; Jefferson to Madison, Oct. 26, 1798, *Republic of Letters*, 2:1077–78.

9. Jefferson to John Taylor, June 1, 1798, in *The Writings of Thomas Jefferson*, ed. Andrew A. Lipscomb and Albert E. Bergh (Washington, DC: Thomas Jefferson Memorial Association, 1903), 10:44–47.

10. Jefferson, "First Inaugural Address," Mar. 4, 1801, *Portable Jefferson*, 292–93.

11. Jefferson, "First Annual Message," Dec. 8, 1801, *Compilation*, 1:314–15.

12. Ibid., 1:316–20.

13. Jefferson, "Second Annual Address," Dec. 15, 1802, *Compilation*, 1:334.

14. Jefferson to John Breckinridge, Aug. 12, 1803, *Portable Jefferson*, 497.

15. Jefferson, "Sixth Annual Address," Dec. 2, 1806, *Compilation*, 1:397–98.

16. See, for example, Jefferson to William H. Cabell, Aug. 7, 11, 17, 1807, Lipscomb and Bergh, *Writings*, 11:307–10, 318–23, 331–32; quote is from letter of Aug. 11.

17. Burton Spivak, *Jefferson's English Crisis: Commerce, Embargo, and the Republican Revolution* (Charlottesville: University of Virginia Press, 1979); Jefferson to James Madison, Aug. 20, 1807, Lipscomb and Bergh, *Writings*, 11:341; Jefferson to Robert Smith, Sept. 3, 1807, Jefferson Papers, Library of Congress; Jefferson to Caesar Rodney, Oct. 8, 1807, quoted in Spivak, *Jefferson's English Crisis*, 85.

18. Jefferson, "Seventh Annual Address," Oct. 27, 1807, *Compilation*, 1:410–16.

19. See Spivak, *Jefferson's English Crisis*, 75–77, 83–84; Albert Gallatin to Thomas Jefferson, Oct. 21, 1807, quoted in Spivak, *Jefferson's English Crisis*, 89; Jefferson to William H. Cabell, Nov. 1, 1807, Lipscomb and Bergh, *Writings*, 11:388–89.

20. Thomas Jefferson to J. W. Eppes, July 12, 1807, in *The Works of Thomas Jefferson*, ed. Paul Leicester Ford (New York: G. P. Putnam's Sons, 1892), 9:457.

21. Jefferson, "Sixth Annual Address," Dec. 2, 1806, *Compilation*, 1:394–95. For details of the trial, see R. Kent Newmyer, *The Treason Trial of Aaron Burr: Law, Politics, and the Character Wars of the New Nation* (New York: Cambridge University Press, 2012).

22. Merrill D. Peterson, *Thomas Jefferson and the New Nation: A Biography* (New York: Oxford University Press, 1970), 851–54, 865–74; Roger G. Kennedy, *Burr, Hamilton, and Jefferson: A Study in Character* (New York: Oxford University Press, 2000), 360; Jefferson to George Hay, May 20, 26, 28, and Sept. 4, 7, 1807, Lipscomb and Bergh, *Writings*, 11:205–6, 209, 210, 360–61, 365; Jefferson to Hay, June 20, 1817, Peterson, *Portable Jefferson*, 507–9.

23. Jefferson to Judge Spencer Roane, Sept. 6, 1819, Peterson, *Writings*, 1426–27; Jefferson to Thomas Ritchie, Dec. 25, 1820, Peterson, *Writings*, 1446.

24. Jefferson to Judge Spencer Roane, Sept. 6, 1819, Peterson, *Writings*, 1426–27; Andrew Jackson quoted in Lincoln, "Speech at Springfield, Illinois," June 26, 1857, *Collected Works*, 2:402.

25. Lincoln, "Address before the Young Men's Lyceum of Springfield, Illinois," Jan. 27, 1838, *Collected Works*, 1:108–115.

26. *Dred Scott v. Sandford* (60 U.S. 393), Cornell University Law School Legal Information Institute, https://www.law.cornell.edu/supremecourt/text/60/393 (accessed Feb. 27, 2015); Lincoln, "Speech at Springfield, Illinois," June 26, 1857, *Collected Works*, 2:400–403.

27. Lincoln to Samuel P. Chase, June 20, 1859, *Collected Works*, 3:386.

28. Lincoln, "Speech at New Haven, Connecticut," Mar. 6, 1860, *Collected Works*, 4:22.

29. Lincoln to William H. Herndon, Feb. 1, 1848, *Collected Works*, 1:446–47.

30. Lincoln to William H. Herndon, Feb. 13, 1848, *Collected Works*, 1:451–52.

31. Lincoln to Herndon, June 22, 1848, *Collected Works*, 1:492; "Speech in U.S. House of Representatives on the Presidential Question," July 27, 1848, *Collected Works*, 1:515.

32. Lincoln to John M. Peck, May 21, 1848, *Collected Works*, 1:473.

33. Lincoln, "Message to Congress in Special Session," July 4, 1861, *Collected Works*, 4:440, 429.

34. Ibid., 4:431–32, 440–41 (emphasis added).

35. *Prize Cases* (67 U.S. 635), Cornell University Law School Legal Information Institute, https://www.law.cornell.edu/supremecourt/text/67/635 (accessed Feb. 27, 2015).

36. A writ of habeas corpus, originating in the 1215 Magna Carta, meant that the government must "produce the body" to prove a murder occurred; more generally over centuries, it came to mean that the government must follow due process in legal situations. For more details about Lincoln's suspension of the writ of habeas corpus, including Chief Justice Taney's views that Lincoln's actions were unconstitutional, see James P. Simon, *Lincoln and Chief Justice Taney* (New York: Simon & Schuster, 2006).

37. Lincoln, "Message to Congress in Special Session," July 4, 1861, *Collected Works*, 4:429–30.

38. Ibid., 4:430–31. Lincoln knew that his attorney general, Edward Bates, would back his position, as Bates did in a speech on July 5, 1861. Congress passed legislation validating the president's actions on March 3, 1863.

39. Lincoln to Erastus Corning and Others, [June 12], 1863, *Collected Works*, 6:264, 267 (emphasis added to last sentence). After the war, the issue of whether a state was subject to actual invasion played a key role in the Supreme Court's decision in *Ex Parte Milligan* (71 U.S. 2 [1866]). By a five-to-four majority, the court ruled that since the authority of the national government had never been challenged in the state of Indiana, and since state courts continued to operate during the Civil War, questions regarding the legitimacy of pleas of habeas corpus had to be decided there rather than by military tribunals. In a dissenting opinion, however, four justices reasoned that a state did not have to actually be invaded in order to fall under Congress's 1863 legislation suspending habeas corpus; see *Ex Parte Milligan*, Cornell University Law School Legal Information Institute, https://www .law.cornell.edu/supremecourt/text/71/2 (accessed May 20, 2015). Based in part on *Milligan*, in *Hamdi v. Rumsfeld* (542 U.S. 507 [2004]), the Supreme Court ruled that a US citizen had the right to a hearing before a court whether or not the "enemy combatant" charge was valid; see *Hamdi v. Rumsfeld*, Cornell University Law School Legal Information Institute, https://www.law.cornell.edu/supct /html/03-6696.ZO.html (accessed May 20, 2015).

40. Lincoln to Erastus Corning and Others, [June 12], 1863, *Collected Works*, 6:265.

41. Lincoln to Orville H. Browning, Sept. 22, 1861, *Collected Works*, 4:531–33.

42. When President Harry S. Truman seized the nation's steel mills in 1950 to avoid strikes, the Supreme Court ruled that the president did not have the right to take private property under either Article II of the Constitution or legislation passed by Congress; see *Youngstown Sheet & Tube v. Sawyer* (343 U.S. 579 [1952]), Justia: US Supreme Court, https://supreme.justia.com/cases/federal/us/343/579/ (accessed May 20, 2015).

6. "SO COMPLICATED A SCIENCE AS POLITICAL ECONOMY"

1. Drew R. McCoy, *The Elusive Republic: Political Economy in Jeffersonian America* (Chapel Hill: University of North Carolina Press, 1980), 7.

2. Jefferson, *Notes, Portable Jefferson*, 217, 227.

3. Jefferson, "First Inaugural Address," *Portable Jefferson*, 293.

4. Jefferson to Benjamin Austin, Jan. 9, 1816, *Portable Jefferson*, 549–50.

5. For Clay's role in defining and shepherding his American System through Congress, see Robert V. Remini, *Henry Clay: Statesman for the Union* (New York: W. W. Norton & Company, 1991), 225–33.

6. See, for example, Lincoln, "Annual Message to Congress, Dec. 1, 1862," *Collected Works*, 5:526.

7. Jean Jacques Rousseau, "A Discourse on Political Economy," in *The Social Contract and Discourses*, trans. G. D. H. Cole (New York: E. P. Dutton and Company, 1950), 288–90.

8. Ibid., 293–95.

9. Ibid., 295, 299–300, 303–6.

10. Ibid., 306–7.

11. Ibid., 307–9.

12. Ibid., 311–2, 316.

13. Ibid., 328, 320, 330.

14. Jefferson, *Notes*, *Portable Jefferson*, 216–17.

15. Ibid., 151–52, 217.

16. Jefferson to James Madison, Dec. 20, 1787, Peterson, *Writings*, 918.

17. Jefferson, *Notes*, *Portable Jefferson*, 217.

18. Jefferson, "First Inaugural Address," Mar. 4, 1801, *Portable Jefferson*, 290, 292.

19. Jefferson, *Notes*, *Portable Jefferson*, 217.

20. Ibid., 226–28, 224.

21. Jefferson, "Second Inaugural Address," Mar. 4, 1805, *Portable Jefferson*, 317.

22. Jefferson, "First Inaugural Address," Mar. 4, 1801, 293.

23. Jefferson, "Second Annual Address," Dec. 15, 1802, *Compilation*, 1:330, 333.

24. Jefferson, "Third Annual Address," Oct. 17, 1803, *Compilation*, 1:348.

25. Jefferson, *Notes*, *Portable Jefferson*, 43–44.

26. Jefferson, "Fourth Annual Address," Nov. 8, 1804, *Compilation*, 1:361.

27. Jefferson, "Second Inaugural Address," Mar. 4, 1805, *Portable Jefferson*, 317. See also "Sixth Annual Address," Dec. 2, 1806, *Compilation*, 1:398.

28. Jefferson, "Sixth Annual Address," Dec. 2, 1806, *Compilation*, 1:398.

29. Jefferson, "Eighth Annual Address," Nov. 8, 1808, *Compilation*, 1:443–44. By the end of his life, Jefferson had tempered his views under the fear that Congress was abusing its powers during the administration of President John Quincy Adams to regulate commerce and to establish post roads to place manufacturing interests over agriculture, to "[cut] down mountains for the construction of roads, of digging canals, and aided by a little sophistry on the words 'general welfare,' a right to do, not only the acts to effect that, which are specifically enumerated and permitted, but whatsoever they shall think, or pretend will be for the general welfare." His remedy for this situation, however, remained amending the Constitution to give Congress the powers to oversee the expansion of internal improvements. Jefferson to William Branch Giles, Dec. 26, 1825, Peterson, *Writings*, 1509–10.

30. Jefferson to General Thaddeus Kosciusko, June 28, 1812, Peterson, *Writings*, 1265.

31. Jefferson to John Melish, Jan. 13, 1813, Peterson, *Writings*, 1267–68.

32. Lincoln, "Communication to the People of Sangamo County," Mar. 9, 1832, *Collected Works*, 1:5–9.

33. Lincoln, "Report and Resolutions Introduced in Illinois Legislature in Relation to Purchase of Public Lands," Jan. 17, 1839, *Collected Works*, 1:135. See also Lincoln, "Remarks in Illinois Legislature Concerning Resolutions in Relation to Purchase of Public Lands," Jan. 17, 1839, *Collected Works*, 1:132–33.

34. Lincoln, "Open Letter on Springfield and Alton Railroad," June 30, 1847, *Collected Works*, 1:395–98.

35. Lincoln, "Speech in United States House of Representatives on Internal Improvements," June 20, 1848, *Collected Works*, 1:483–84.

36. Lincoln, "Fragments of a Tariff Discussion," [Dec. 1, 1847?], *Collected Works*, 1:407–12 (brackets added by Basler except in the last case). See also Lincoln, "Speech at Peoria, Illinois," Sept. 17, 1852, 2:158.

37. Richard Hofstadter, "Abraham Lincoln and the Self-Made Myth," in *The American Political Tradition and the Men Who Made It* (New York: Random House, 1948), 105.

38. Lincoln, "Fragment on Free Labor," [Sept. 17, 1859?], *Collected Works*, 3:462–63.

39. Lincoln, "Address before the Wisconsin State Agricultural Society, Milwaukee, Wisconsin," Sept. 30, 1859, *Collected Works*, 3:479. See also Lincoln, "Speech at Hartford, Connecticut," Mar. 5, 1860, *Collected Works*, 4:7–8; "Speech at New Haven, Connecticut," Mar. 6, 1860, *Collected Works*, 4:2–30; and "Annual Message to Congress," Dec. 3, 1861, *Collected Works*, 5:52.

40. Lincoln, "Autobiography Written for John L. Scripps," [c. June 1860], *Collected Works*, 4:62.

41. Lincoln, "Communication to the People of Sangamo County," Mar. 9, 1832, *Collected Works*, 1:8.

42. Lincoln, "Eulogy on Henry Clay," July 6, 1852, *Collected Works*, 2:124, 126.

43. Lincoln, "Address before the Wisconsin State Agricultural Society, Milwaukee, Wisconsin," Sept. 30, 1859, *Collected Works*, 3:476–77, 480–81 (emphasis added).

44. Lincoln, "Annual Message to Congress," Dec. 3, 1861, *Collected Works*, 5:46.

45. Lincoln, "Annual Message to Congress," Dec. 6, 1864, *Collected Works*, 8:147–48.

46. "About the Land Grant System," West Virginia Extension Service, http://www.ext.wvu.edu/about_extension/land_grant_system (accessed Feb. 23, 2015) (emphasis added).

47. Ibid.

48. Ibid. (emphasis added).

49. Jefferson, *Notes*, *Portable Jefferson*, 193–97.

50. Jefferson to James Madison, Dec. 20, 1787, Peterson, *Writings*, 918; Jefferson, *Notes*, *Portable Jefferson*, 197–99.

51. Jefferson, *Notes*, *Portable Jefferson*, 214; Jefferson to Wilson Cary Nicholas, Apr. 2, 1816, Lipscomb and Bergh, *Writings*, 14:451–54. See also Jefferson to Joseph C. Cabell, Feb. 2, 1816, Peterson, *Writings*, 1380–81.

52. Jefferson, "Report of the Commissioners for the University of Virginia," Aug. 4, 1818, *Portable Jefferson*, 333–35.

53. Jefferson to Horatio G. Spafford, Mar. 17, 1814, Lipscomb and Bergh, *Writings*, 14:20; Jefferson, "Report of the Commissioners for the University of Virginia," Aug. 4, 1818, *Portable Jefferson*, 334–35.

54. McCoy, *Elusive Republic*, 248–50. Historian Allen Guelzo takes a similar position in chapter 1 of *Abraham Lincoln*.

55. Jefferson, *Notes*, *Portable Jefferson*, 215.

56. Lincoln, "Annual Message to Congress," Dec. 3, 1861, *Collected Works*, 5:52–53.

57. Rousseau, "Discourse," 291; Jefferson, "To Nehemiah Dodge and Others, a Committee of the Danbury Baptist Association, in the State of Connecticut," Jan. 1,

1802, *Portable Jefferson*, 304; Lincoln, "First Inaugural Address," Mar. 4, 1861, *Collected Works*, 4:270.

58. Jefferson, "Report of the Commissioners for the University of Virginia," Aug. 4, 1818, *Portable Jefferson*, 335. In a similar way, Jefferson proposed creating a national university in order to stimulate scientific education in the nation, but Congress failed to act on his request. Jefferson, "Sixth Annual Address," Dec. 2, 1806, *Compilation*, 1:398.

59. "About the Land Grant System," West Virginia Extension Service, http://www.ext.wvu.edu/about_extension/land_grant_system (accessed Feb. 23, 2015).

60. Lincoln, "Address before the Wisconsin State Agricultural Society, Milwaukee, Wisconsin," Sept. 30, 1859, *Collected Works*, 3:481; Jefferson, *Notes, Portable Jefferson*, 198–99; Lincoln, "Address Delivered at the Dedication of the Cemetery at Gettysburg," Nov. 19, 1863, *Collected Works*, 7:23.

EPILOGUE: JEFFERSON, LINCOLN, AND
THE IMPORTANCE OF PLACE

1. Jefferson to James Monroe, June 17, 1785, *Portable Jefferson*, 377.
2. Jefferson to [Baron von Geismar], Sept. 6, 1785, *Papers*, 1:379.
3. Jefferson to Maria Cosway, Oct. 12, 1786, *Portable Jefferson*, 404.
4. Jefferson to Martha Jefferson Randolph, May 31, 1791, *Family Letters*, 454–58.
5. Jefferson to Chastellux, Sept. 2, 1785, *Portable Jefferson*, 386–88.
6. Robert Beverley, *The History and Present State of Virginia, in Four Parts* (1705; repr., Chapel Hill: University of North Carolina Press, 1947), 296.
7. Jack P. Greene, "The Intellectual Reconstruction of Virginia in the Age of Jefferson," *William and Mary Quarterly*, 3rd ser., 16 (1959): 226.
8. Jefferson, *Notes, Portable Jefferson*, 215, 217.
9. Jefferson to Pierre Samuel du Pont de Nemours, Mar. 2, 1809, Lipscomb and Bergh, *Writings*, 12:259–60; Jefferson to John Armstrong, Mar. 5, 1809, Lipscomb and Bergh, *Writings*, 12:262; Jefferson to Alexander von Humbolt, Mar. 6, 1809, in *The Papers of Thomas Jefferson: Retirement Series*, ed. J. Jefferson Looney (Princeton, NJ: Princeton University Press, 2004), 1:24.
10. Jefferson to Samuel Kercheval, July 12, 1816, *Portable Jefferson*, 552–53.
11. Lincoln to Jesse W. Fell, "Enclosing Autobiography," Dec. 20, 1859, *Collected Works*, 3:512.
12. Lincoln, "Communication to the People of Sangamo County," Mar. 9, 1832, *Collected Works*, 1:5–8.
13. Lincoln, "To the Editor of the *Sangamo Journal*," June 13, 1836, *Collected Works*, 1:48.
14. Lincoln, "Discussion in Illinois Legislature concerning the Division of Sangamon County," Dec. 21, 1836, *Collected Works*, 1:56; "Amendments Introduced in Illinois Legislature to Senate Bill Permanently Locating the Seat of Government of the State of Illinois," [Feb. 14, 1837], *Collected Works*, 1:73; "Remarks in Illinois Legislature concerning Appropriation for Building the State House," Jan. 7, 1839, *Collected Works*, 1:126–27.

15. Lincoln to Joshua Speed, Oct. 22, 1846, *Collected Works*, 1:391; Lincoln to William H. Herndon, Jan. 8, 1848, *Collected Works*, 1:430.
16. Lincoln to Jesse Lynch, Apr. 10, 1848, *Collected Works*, 1:463–64.
17. See, for example, Douglas L. Wilson, *Lincoln's Sword: The Presidency and the Power of Words* (New York: Knopf, 2006), 37–38.
18. Lincoln, "'A House Divided': Speech at Springfield, Illinois," June 16, 1858, *Collected Works*, 2:465, 467.
19. See, for example, Lincoln, "Sixth Debate with Stephen A. Douglas at Quincy, Illinois," Oct. 13, 1858, *Collected Works*, 3:246–47.
20. Lincoln, "Fourth Debate with Stephen A. Douglas at Charleston, Illinois," Sept. 18, 1858, *Collected Works*, 3:179. See also Lincoln, "Fifth Debate with Stephen A. Douglas," Oct. 7, 1858, *Collected Works*, 3:221, and "Sixth Debate with Stephen A. Douglas at Quincy, Illinois," Oct. 13, 1858, *Collected Works*, 3:248–50.
21. Wilson, *Lincoln's Sword*; Lincoln, "Seventh and Last Debate with Stephen A. Douglas at Alton, Illinois," Oct. 15, 1858, *Collected Works*, 3:300.
22. Lincoln, "Speech at Chicago, Illinois," Mar. 1, 1859, *Collected Works*, 3:367, 370.
23. Lincoln to Theodore Canisius, May 17, 1859, *Collected Works*, 3:380.
24. Lincoln to Schuyler Colfax, July 6, 1859, *Collected Works*, 3:391. See also Lincoln, "Speech at Cincinnati, Ohio," Sept. 17, 1859, *Collected Works*, 3:461.
25. Lincoln, "Address at Cooper Institute, New York City," Feb. 27, 1860, *Collected Works*, 3:547–50.
26. Lincoln to Mark W. Delahay, May 14, 1859, *Collected Works*, 3:379 (second set of brackets added by Basler).
27. Lincoln, "Address at Cooper Institute, New York City," Feb. 27, 1860, *Collected Works*, 3:535.
28. Lincoln, "Remarks at Springfield, Illinois," Nov. 20, 1860, *Collected Works*, 4:142; "Remarks at Bloomington, Illinois," Nov. 21, 1860, *Collected Works*, 4:144.
29. Lincoln, "Speech at Lafayette, Indiana," Feb. 11, 1861, *Collected Works*, 4:192.
30. Lincoln, "First Inaugural Address—Final Text," Mar. 4, 1861, *Collected Works*, 4:268, 270–71.
31. Lincoln, "Response to a Serenade," Nov. 10, 1864, *Collected Works*, 8:101.
32. Lincoln, "Second Inaugural Address," Mar. 4, 1865, *Collected Works*, 8:332–33.
33. Wills, *Lincoln at Gettysburg*, 187.
34. See Hatzenbuehler, *"I Tremble for My Country,"* 145.
35. Lincoln, "Second Inaugural Address," Mar. 4, 1865, *Collected Works*, 8:333. Historian Eric Foner also emphasizes the fact that Lincoln's "contact with new people, new ideas, and a totally unprecedented situation [allowed him] to make the most of these encounters." Eric Foner, *The Fiery Trial: Abraham Lincoln and American Slavery* (New York: W. W. Norton & Co., 2010), xx. Whereas Foner has Lincoln ending his life as a Northerner, I argue that at the time of his death, he was a nationalist who envisioned a reconciliation between the North and the South.

36. For Jefferson's views of women's limited roles in society, see Jan Lewis, *The Pursuit of Happiness: Family and Values in Jefferson's Virginia* (New York: Cambridge University Press, 1983) and Jon Kukla, *Mr. Jefferson's Women* (New York: Viking Books, 2008). Lincoln's papers contain no reference to the Seneca Falls Convention (1848) or to subsequent annual women's rights conventions. Resolutions presented to the 1864 convention pledged support for complete emancipation of slaves, and the final resolution stated, "There never can be a true peace in this Republic until the civil and political rights of all citizens of African descent and all women are practically established." Some attending the convention deemed the resolution supporting women's rights too radical and fretted that it would compromise the goal of equal rights for former slaves; it was defeated. National Park Service, "More Women's Rights Conventions," http://www.nps.gov/wori/learn/historyculture /more-womens-rights-conventions.htm (accessed Nov. 13, 2015).

POSTSCRIPT

1. On dealings with the Supreme Court, see Newmyer, *Treason Trial of Aaron Burr*, and Simon, *Lincoln and Chief Justice Taney*; on views of the West, see Donald Jackson, *Thomas Jefferson and the Stony Mountains: Exploring the West from Monticello* (Champaign: University of Illinois Press, 1981) and Richard W. Etulain, ed., *Lincoln Looks West: From the Mississippi to the Pacific* (Carbondale: Southern Illinois University Press, 2010); on their relationships with cabinet members, see Noble E. Cunningham Jr., *The Jeffersonian Republicans in Power: Party Operations, 1801–1809* (Chapel Hill: University of North Carolina Press, 1963) and Doris Kearns Goodwin, *Team of Rivals: The Political Genius of Abraham Lincoln* (New York: Simon & Schuster, 2005).

2. Jefferson, "A Memorandum (Services to My Country)," [c. 1800], Peterson, *Writings*, 703.

3. Lincoln, "Application for Patent on an Improved Method of Lifting Vessels over Shoals," Mar. 10, 1849, *Collected Works*, 2:32–36; Jason Emerson, *Lincoln the Inventor* (Carbondale: Southern Illinois University Press, 2009).

───────────────{ A Note on Sources }───────────────

I have relied throughout this work on the two men's primary sources, including their letters, speeches, official state papers, and writings. In years past, it was not uncommon to see a book such as *Speak for Yourself, Daniel: A Life of Daniel Webster in His Own Words* (Boston: Houghton-Mifflin, 1969), meaning that pulling together selected primary sources and arranging them chronologically would bring the person to life, as it were. While I would not be so bold as to believe that I have written such a book, each chapter traces the development, maturation, and sometimes changes in Jefferson's and Lincoln's ideas over time and concludes with a comparison of their thoughts. Although I have employed a thematic approach, I do not consider the book to be heavily analytical in the sense of seeing where current scholarship stands on a particular topic and trying to integrate my slant into that literature. As a case in point, my prior monograph on Jefferson employed just such an approach—that is, that he is best viewed from a local rather than a national or even international perspective. Periodically in the text, I cite a secondary source to indicate where my views coincide with or diverge from other interpretations, but I have not located this work within the massive literature on these two individuals. For readable biographies of the two individuals, I suggest, on Jefferson, two texts by Merrill D. Peterson, the concise introduction to *Portable Jefferson* and the longer *Thomas Jefferson and the New Nation: A Biography*; and on Lincoln, the concise work by James M. McPherson, *Abraham Lincoln* (New York: Oxford University Press, 2009), and the longer books by David Donald, *Lincoln*, and Ronald C. White Jr., *A. Lincoln: A Biography*.

Although most of the documents that I have chosen may be found readily on the Internet, for the most part I have cited them in accessible compilations of Jefferson's and Lincoln's works so that readers may explore for themselves the power of the two men's word choices. I have preserved the spelling and punctuation of the originals (including both men's common use of the spelling "it's" instead of "its" for the possessive) except where it was necessary to clarify context or, in the case of *Portable Jefferson*, where modernized spelling and punctuation appear in the work being cited. Retaining Abraham Lincoln's punctuation is especially important because he designed his speeches as much for the hearer as for the reader, or more.

With regard to Jefferson's texts, two compilations edited by Merrill D. Peterson contain the lion's share of the materials I have used: *The Portable Thomas Jefferson* and *Thomas Jefferson: Writings*. In places, however, I have found it necessary to supplement the contents of these works with excerpts from *The Papers of Thomas Jefferson*, edited by Julian P. Boyd; *The Works of Thomas Jefferson*, edited by Paul Leicester Ford; *The Writings of Thomas Jefferson*, edited by Andrew A. Lipscomb and Albert E. Bergh; and other collections.

For Lincoln, there are two notable brief collections: *Abraham Lincoln, Slavery, and the Civil War: Selected Writings and Speeches*, edited by Michael P. Johnson; and *The Portable Abraham Lincoln*, edited by Andrew Delbanco. However, I have cited Lincoln's materials using the standard compilation edited by Roy P. Basler, *The Collected Works of Abraham Lincoln*.

Recent biographies of Lincoln have relied on recollections of his associates as reproduced in two books: Douglas L. Wilson and Rodney D. Davis, eds., *Herndon's Informants: Letters, Interviews, and Statements about Abraham Lincoln* (Champaign: University of Illinois Press, 1997); and Don and Virginia Fehrenbacher, eds., *Recollected Words of Abraham Lincoln* (Palo Alto, CA: Stanford University Press, 1998). Although most of these accounts are firsthand, many of them are contradictory or cannot be attributed to a specific time or place; therefore, I have chosen for the most part not to rely on them. Readers who want to see how scholars have used these reminiscences and anecdotes to probe Lincoln's personality or actions should consult, for example, Ronald White Jr.'s *A. Lincoln: A Biography*, Michael Burlingame's *Abraham Lincoln: A Life* (Baltimore: Johns Hopkins University Press, 2008), or Eric Foner's monograph on Lincoln's changing views on slavery, *The Fiery Trial: Abraham Lincoln and American Slavery*.

Ronald L. Hatzenbuehler is a professor emeritus of history at Idaho State University. He is the recipient of numerous awards for teaching, including ISU's Distinguished Teacher Award (1994) and the Idaho Humanities Council's Outstanding Achievement in the Humanities Award (2008). His previous publications consist of numerous articles on early US history, as well as the books *"I Tremble for My Country": Thomas Jefferson and the Virginia Gentry* and, as coauthor, *Congress Declares War: Rhetoric, Leadership, and Partisanship in the Early Republic.*